WOK
C·O·O·K·I·N·G

Y0-CDJ-490

GOLDEN APPLE PUBLISHERS

WOK COOKING

A GOLDEN APPLE PUBLICATION/
PUBLISHED BY ARRANGEMENT WITH OTTENHEIMER PUBLISHERS INC.

JUNE 1986

GOLDEN APPLE IS A TRADEMARK OF GOLDEN APPLE PUBLISHERS

ISBN 0-553-19857-2
Printed in Korea

Contents

Appetizers

Cantonese Steamed Pork Dumplings

2	stalks bok choy (or Chinese celery cabbage)
1	pound boneless pork shoulder, finely ground
1	tablespoon Chinese rice wine or pale dry sherry
1	tablespoon soy sauce

2	teaspoons salt
1	teaspoon sugar
1	tablespoon cornstarch
¼	cup canned bamboo shoots, finely chopped
	Dumpling and Bun Dough (see Index)

With a cleaver or heavy, sharp knife, trim wilted leaves and root ends from the bok choy. Wash the stalks under cold running water, drain, and chop finely. Squeeze the chopped cabbage in a kitchen towel or double layer of cheesecloth to extract as much of its moisture as possible.

Combine the pork, wine, soy sauce, salt, sugar, and cornstarch, and, with a large spoon, mix them thoroughly together. Stir in the cabbage and bamboo shoots. Place a spoonful of filling in the center of a dough circle and fold into a dumpling suitable for steaming.

Pour enough water into the base of the wok to come within an inch of the bamboo steamer and bring to a boil. Place the dumplings into as many steamer racks as are needed to hold them and steam for 30 minutes. Add water as needed. Serve the dumplings directly on the steamer plate set on a platter. Makes about 48 dumplings.

Dumpling and Bun Dough

Unleavened Dough
2   cups all-purpose flour,
    sifted
¾   cup cold water

Leavened Dough
¼   cup sugar

½   cup milk, room
    temperature
½   regular small cake of yeast
1   tablespoon lard or
    hydrogenated shortening
2   cups all-purpose flour,
    sifted

To make unleavened dough circles: Mix flour and water with your hands or a large spoon in a mixing bowl until dough becomes stiff. Knead dough until smooth and let stand for 30 minutes. Roll with a rolling pin into a smooth sheet about 1/8-inch thick. Stamp out circles about 3 inches in diameter with a cookie cutter. This is then ready to be wrapped around a filling.

To make leavened dough circles: Mix sugar and milk with the yeast and let stand at room temperature for 20 minutes. Chop lard into small pieces, add it to the flour, and add both to the milk mixture. Cover and allow to rise in a warm place. When volume has nearly doubled, knead again, and let stand for another 40 minutes. Then use to make dough circles much like those done with the unleavened dough. Makes about 48 dumplings or buns.

Folding a dumpling or bun for steaming: Place a spoonful of filling in center of dough circle. Gather sides of wrapper around filling, letting them pleat naturally. Squeeze center of the now-cylindrical dumpling to pack filling tightly. Tap dumpling lightly to flatten its bottom and make it stand upright.

Folding a dumpling for frying or boiling: Place a spoonful of filling into center of dough circle. Fold circle in half across filling and pinch it together at the center. Make 3 or 4 pleats at each end to gather dough around filling. Pinch along top of dumpling to seal edges tightly together.

Folding Buns: Place a spoonful of filling into center of dough circle. Gather edges of dough up around filling in loose, natural folds. Bring folds up to top of the ball and twist securely together. Set bun aside with its twisted side up. You may roll bun between the palms of your hands to turn it into a smooth ball.

After you fill the dumplings or buns, and before boiling, steaming, or frying, they should be set aside, covered, for 15 minutes.

Steamed Dumplings

Indian Spiced Ground Beef Dumplings

1 large onion, chopped	**Dumpling and Bun Dough**
2 tablespoons vegetable oil	**(see Index)**
1 pound lean ground beef	1 egg, lightly beaten
1 tablespoon curry powder	2 to 3 cups of oil for frying
1 teaspoon paprika	
½ teaspoon chili powder (or	*Mustard Sauce*
1 teaspoon red pepper	2 tablespoons mustard
flakes if you like hot	4 tablespoons cold water
foods)	½ teaspoon vinegar
¼ teaspoon black pepper	¼ teaspoon salt
½ teaspoon garlic salt	¼ teaspoon brown sugar
2 fresh medium tomatoes,	
diced	*Curry Powder*
Salt to taste	½ cup ground coriander
1 (8½-ounce) can peas	¼ cup ground cumin
	¼ cup ground turmeric
	¼ cup ground ginger

Sauté onion in oil in the wok until golden brown. Mix beef, spices, tomatoes, salt, and peas thoroughly, using some of the liquid from the can. Add sautéed onion, and mix. Place a spoonful of the mixture into center of a dough circle and fold for frying. Seal with the beaten egg and set on oiled waxed paper until ready to cook.

Heat 2 to 3 cups oil to 350°F. Deep-fry dumplings for 2 to 3 minutes, until golden brown; drain and serve hot with mustard sauce or curry powder. Makes about 48 dumplings.

To make mustard sauce, in a small bowl combine mustard with half the water. Stir to a smooth paste. Stir in vinegar, salt, brown sugar, and, finally, in a thin stream, the remaining water. Store in the refrigerator. (Makes about 1/4 cup.)

To make curry powder, mix ingredients well and bottle tightly. (Makes 1-1/4 cups.)

Deep-Fried Date Buns

1 pound dates, pitted	2 to 3 cups oil for frying
1 cup walnuts, shelled	Confectioners' sugar
4 tablespoons frozen orange	Dumpling and Bun Dough
juice concentrate	(see Index)
4 tablespoons orange rind,	
grated	

Delicious Pineapple Spareribs

Cut dates into chunks about 1-inch square. Place 1/4 of the dates and 1/4 of the walnuts in blender. At high speed, blend into finest particles. Turn into a large bowl, add orange juice and rind, and knead into a large ball. Place a spoonful of fruit mixture into the center of a dough circle and twist into bun form. Roll in hands until smooth.

Heat oil in wok to 375°F. Fry buns 6 to 8 at a time until just golden brown. Drain well, cool, and sprinkle lightly with confectioners' sugar before serving. Makes about 48 buns.

Steamed Date Buns

½ **cup lard or hydrogenated shortening**	**Red food coloring (optional)**
2 **cups canned red-bean paste**	**Dumpling and Bun Dough (see Index)**
1 **pound pitted dates, finely chopped**	

Melt lard in wok at moderate heat, add canned bean paste and chopped dates, and cook, stirring constantly, for 8 to 10 minutes. Transfer contents of wok to a bowl and cool thoroughly.

Place a spoonful of the mixture into center of a dough circle and twist into a bun form. Roll in your hands until a smooth ball is formed. Steam smooth buns in bamboo steamer trays above boiling water in the base of the wok for 10 minutes. Serve hot directly in the steamer tray placed on a pan. Makes about 48 buns.

Northern-Style Pork Dumplings

½ **pound bok choy (or Chinese celery cabbage)**	2 **tablespoons peanut or vegetable oil**
1 **pound lean boneless pork, finely ground**	**Dumpling and Bun Dough (see Index)**
1 **teaspoon fresh gingerroot, grated**	1 **cup chicken broth, fresh or canned**
1 **tablespoon Chinese rice wine, or pale dry sherry**	¼ **cup soy sauce combined with 2 tablespoons white vinegar (to be used as a dip or sauce)**
1 **tablespoon soy sauce**	
1 **teaspoon salt**	
1 **tablespoon sesame seed oil**	

With a cleaver or heavy, sharp knife, trim wilted leaves and root ends from bok choy, and separate cabbage into stalks. Wash stalks under cold running water, drain, and chop finely. Squeeze chopped cabbage in a kitchen towel or double layer of cheesecloth to extract as much of its moisture as possible.

Combine ground pork, chopped gingerroot, wine, soy sauce, salt, and sesame seed oil, and then add chopped cabbage. Mix with your hands or a large spoon until ingredients are thoroughly blended. This mixture can then be used as a filling for dumplings, folded and sealed for boiling or frying.

To boil: Bring 2 quarts of water to boiling in wok and drop in dumplings. Stir to make sure dumplings are not sticking together. Boil for 10 to 15 minutes, adding additional water as needed. Serve dumplings hot with soy sauce and vinegar dip.

Chinese Soup

To fry: Place 2 tablespoons of oil into wok and swirl it about. Place dumplings, pleated-side up, into wok and cook until bottoms brown lightly (about 2 minutes at low heat). Add chicken broth, cover tightly, and cook until it has been absorbed (about 10 minutes). Add remaining 1 tablespoon of oil and fry each dumpling at least another 2 minutes. Serve fried dumplings hot with soy sauce and vinegar dip. Makes about 48 dumplings.

Vietnamese Fried Dumplings

12	dried Chinese mushrooms (optional)
2	eggs, slightly beaten
1	tablespoon vegetable oil
1	tablespoon fish sauce or soy sauce
1	tablespoon lemon juice, strained
½	teaspoon salt
⅛	teaspoon black pepper
Pinch of chili powder (or 1 teaspoon red pepper flakes if you like hot foods)	
1	small onion, minced
1	cup ground, lean pork
1	cup cooked vermicelli, minced, or cooked rice
1	clove garlic, peeled and minced
2	cups raw shrimp, shelled, deveined, and minced
1	cup bean sprouts, rinsed

Dumpling and Bun Dough (see Index)

3 cups oil (for deep-fat frying)

Shredded lettuce

Sweet-and-Sour Sauce (see Index)

Soak mushrooms in warm water for 20 minutes, drain, and mince. Place in a medium bowl and mix with 1/2 the egg, 1 tablespoon oil, fish (or soy) sauce, lemon juice, salt, pepper, chili powder (or red pepper), onion, pork, vermicelli (or rice), garlic, shrimp, and bean sprouts. Place a spoonful of this mixture into the center of a dough circle and fold into a dumpling suitable for frying. Seal with rest of beaten egg and set on oiled waxed paper until ready to cook.

Add 3 cups of oil to wok and heat to 350°F. Deep-fry dumplings for 2 to 3 minutes, until golden brown; drain, and serve hot with shredded lettuce and Sweet-and-Sour Sauce. Makes about 48 dumplings.

Sweet-and-Sour Chinese Meatballs

1	pound extra-lean ground beef
¾	teaspoon salt
½	teaspoon pepper
½	teaspoon fresh gingerroot, grated
2	tablespoons vegetable oil
1	green pepper, cut into ¼-inch cubes
1	onion, chopped
1	carrot, grated
2	tablespoons vinegar
2	tablespoons brown sugar
1	teaspoon soy sauce
1	teaspoon dry sherry
1	tablespoon cornstarch stirred into ½ cup cold chicken or beef broth

Blend ground beef, salt, pepper, and ginger together. Shape into 1-inch meatballs. Heat oil in wok and brown meatballs on all sides for about 2 minutes. Add all remaining ingredients. Cook over moderate heat, stirring constantly, until mixture thickens. Cook an additional 5 minutes. Serve at once with rice. Makes 4 servings.

Corn and Chicken Soup

Hong-Kong Meatballs

1½ pounds ground beef
½ cup celery, very finely chopped
1 teaspoon seasoned salt
1 teaspoon soy sauce
1 tablespoon vegetable oil
¼ cup bamboo shoots, thinly sliced
1 (1-pound) can mixed Chinese vegetables or bean sprouts, drained, with liquid reserved
1 green pepper, seeded and cut in julienne strips
1 carrot, peeled and shredded
1 (5-ounce) can water chestnuts, drained and thinly sliced
1½ tablespoons cornstarch
2 teaspoons (additional) soy sauce
2 teaspoons sherry
¼ cup slivered almonds, blanched

Mix ground beef with celery, seasoned salt, and soy sauce. Mix thoroughly to blend all ingredients, then shape into 1-inch-diameter meatballs.

Heat vegetable oil in a wok and sauté meatballs over high heat until browned on all sides. Stir in bamboo shoots; cover and simmer 5 minutes, stirring occasionally. At the end of cooking time, pour off any accumulated fat.

Add drained Chinese vegetables, green pepper strips, shredded carrot, and water chestnuts; stir well. In a 2-cup measure, mix cornstarch, soy sauce, and sherry until a thin paste is formed. Add liquid from Chinese vegetables and enough water to make 2 cups in all. Add to meatballs and cook uncovered for 5 to 10 minutes, stirring occasionally, until sauce is thickened. Sprinkle with almonds before serving. Makes 6 servings.

Barbequed Pork

1 clove garlic
2 slices fresh gingerroot
3 tablespoons brown sugar
2 tablespoons dry sherry
4 tablespoons soy sauce
½ teaspoon 5-spices powder
½ teaspoon red food coloring
2 scallions, thinly sliced
¼ cup chicken stock
2 pounds lean pork butt or shoulder, boned and sliced into 2-inch-thick slices

Combine all ingredients except pork and bring to a simmering temperature. Place pork in a shallow bowl and cover with warmed marinade. Cover and refrigerate overnight. Turn slices occasionally to be sure all have equal exposure to marinade.

Remove pork and place on a rack over a dripping pan. Baste well with marinade. Roast in a 325°F oven for 1-1/2 hours, basting often with marinade and drippings.

Peking Egg Drop Soup

To serve warm, cut the thick slices into 1/8-inch-thin slices and arrange on a platter. Pour over some of the warm marinade. To serve cold, allow meat to cool in the marinade, slice thinly, and serve with or without the marinade as a sauce. Makes 8 to 12 servings.

Water Chestnuts with Bacon

⅓ to ½ **pound bacon**	1 **tablespoon soy sauce**
1 **(6-ounce) can of water**	1 **tablespoon dry sherry**
chestnuts	
Toothpicks	

Wrap 1/2 slice of bacon around each water chestnut and fasten with a toothpick. Place water chestnuts in an ovenproof dish and brush with a mixture of soy sauce and sherry. Bake at 350°F for 15 to 20 minutes. Makes about 20 appetizers.

Shrimp Puffs

1 pound shrimp, cleaned, deveined, very finely chopped	1 teaspoon cornstarch
	2 teapoons dry sherry
	1 teaspoon soy sauce
8 to 9 water chestnuts, minced	2 cups oil for frying
1 egg, beaten	Lemon wedges and soy sauce
1 teaspoon salt	for dipping
½ teaspoon sugar	

Combine shrimp, water chestnuts, egg, salt, sugar, cornstarch, sherry, and soy sauce. Heat oil in wok to 375°F. Shape shrimp mixture into balls the size of small walnuts and drop from a spoon into the hot oil. Fry until the balls float and turn pink and golden. Drain on paper towels.

Serve hot with lemon wedges and a bowl of soy sauce for dipping. Makes about 16 puffs.

Delicious Pineapple Spareribs

4 pounds pork spareribs	½ cup oil
1 cup vinegar	1 (15-ounce) can pineapple
8 tablespoons cornstarch	pieces
½ cup brown sugar	½ cup water
2 tablespoons soy sauce	1 large carrot

Chop spareribs into individual ribs. Put ribs into a wok with 4 tablespoons of vinegar and enough water to cover. Bring to a boil, simmer for 5 minutes, then drain.

Mix cornstarch with 1/2 of the sugar and the soy sauce. Coat ribs in this mixture. Heat oil in a wok and fry ribs until browned. Remove and drain on paper towels.

Drain pineapple pieces. Put 1/2 cup of syrup in wok with the water, remaining sugar, and remaining vinegar. Bring to a boil, then add spareribs; cover and simmer for 20 minutes.

Cut carrot into long, thin strips and add to wok with the pineapple pieces. Simmer a further 5 minutes. Makes 4 to 6 servings.

Soups

Imitation Bird's Nest or Long-Rice Soup

1 cup soaked long rice (½ bunch—available in Oriental-food stores)	½ tablespoon soy sauce
¾ teaspoon salt	1 teaspoon (or ½ cup, optional) green onions (with tops), finely chopped
5 cups boiling water or chicken broth	½ cup mushrooms, finely chopped (optional)
⅜ cup fresh lean pork, finely minced	½ cup bamboo shoots (optional), finely chopped
⅓ cup smoked ham, finely minced	¼ teaspoon cornstarch (optional)
1 tablespoon water chestnuts, finely chopped	

Soak long rice in cold water for 1/2 hour. Drain and cut in 6-inch lengths. Add long rice and salt to boiling water and boil for 20 minutes. Combine pork, ham, water chestnuts, and soy sauce. Shape into balls 3/4 inch in diameter. Drop into soup mixture and boil 10 minutes. Do not stir. Add green onions and serve immediately. To improve the flavor, 1/2 cup finely chopped mushrooms and 1/2 cup finely chopped bamboo shoots may be added to the soup and the green onions increased to 1/2 cup.

One-fourth teaspoon cornstarch may be mixed with the soy sauce and meat mixture so that the balls will retain their shape during cooking. Makes 6 to 8 servings.

Chinese Soup

1 quart chicken broth	2 ounces cooked ham, cut into thin strips
½ teaspoon salt (or salt to taste)	2 ounces cooked chicken, cut into thin strips
¼ teaspoon pepper (or less)	
2 teaspoons soy sauce	
2 ounces whole, cooked shrimp	

Bring chicken broth to a boil and add all the remaining ingredients. Simmer 3 to 4 minutes and serve immediately. Makes 4 to 6 servings.

Clam Soup

1 dozen large, fresh clams	1 teaspoon soy sauce
5 cups water	2 tablespoons dry sherry
1 teaspoon salt	1 scallion, sliced

Scrub the clams with a stiff brush to remove all sand and debris. Drop the clams into boiling water and boil just until the shells have opened. Remove from heat and discard the shells. Add the salt, soy sauce, and dry sherry to the broth. Place 3 or 4 clams in each bowl. Add the broth, and garnish with scallion slices. Makes 3 or 4 servings.

Corn and Chicken Soup

6 ounces raw chicken meat, minced	1 (10-ounce) can cream-style corn
1 tablespoon dry sherry	2 tablespoons cornstarch in ¼ cup cold water
1 teaspoon salt	Thin strips of ham
2 egg whites	
1 quart chicken broth	

Combine chicken with sherry, salt, and egg whites. Bring chicken broth to a full, rolling boil. Add minced-chicken mixture and corn. Simmer 2 minutes. Add cornstarch mixture and simmer an additional 2 minutes, stirring continuously. Add more salt, if needed. Pour into serving bowls and garnish with thin strips of ham. Makes 4 to 6 servings.

Oriental Soup

Chicken Soup

2	**(5-ounce) cans boned chicken**
5	**cups chicken broth (use the liquid from the boned chicken as part of this liquid)**

1	**(4-ounce) can mushroom stems and pieces, drained and liquid reserved**
2	**teaspoons soy sauce**
2	**cups fine egg noodles**
4	**thin slices lemon with rind**

Put chicken and broth in wok. Cover and bring slowly to a boil. Add mushrooms, soy sauce, and noodles. Stir and cook until noodles are done. Garnish with lemon rind. Makes 4 to 6 servings.

Celery Cabbage and Shrimp Soup

1 **small head celery cabbage**	1 **tablespoon vegetable oil**
5 **water chestnuts**	3½ **cups boiling water**
½ **cup large dried or 1 cup canned shrimp**	1 **teaspoon salt**
1 **cup water**	4 **green onions (with tops), finely chopped**

Wash and cut cabbage crosswise into 1-inch strips. Wash, peel, and cut water chestnuts crosswise into 1/4-inch slices. Soak dried shrimp in 1 cup water for 1/2 hour. Drain shrimp, but save the liquid. Heat oil until it is very hot, add shrimp, and fry for 2 to 3 minutes. Add shrimp liquid, water chestnuts, 3-1/2 cups boiling water, and salt. Bring liquid to the boiling point and simmer for 1/2 hour. Add cabbage and boil for 5 to 10 minutes, until cabbage is tender but has not lost all its crispness. Add finely chopped green onions and serve hot.

If wet-packed shrimp are used, substitute 2/3 cup liquid from the canned shrimp for 2/3 cup water. Clean shrimp by removing the black vein along the back. Makes 6 servings.

Cucumber Soup

¾ **tablespoon salt**	10 **medium-sized mushrooms, cut into ½-inch strips**
¼ **teaspoon cornstarch**	5 **red dates, if desired**
1 **teaspoon soy sauce**	¾ **cup bamboo shoots, sliced in pieces ½ × ¼ × ¾ inch**
½ **cup pork, sliced in pieces ½ × ¼ × ¾ inch**	3 **cucumbers**
1 **tablespoon vegetable oil**	**Fish balls (optional)**
4 **cups water**	

Add 1/4 teaspoon salt, cornstarch, and soy sauce to pork and allow them to stand for 5 minutes. Heat oil and brown pork for 3 minutes. Add water, mushrooms, red dates, bamboo shoots, and remaining salt, and simmer for 30 to 45 minutes. Discard red dates. Peel cucumbers and cut them into cross sections. Add cucumber pieces to soup and boil it for 3 minutes. Serve immediately.

Fish balls may be added. Drop them into the boiling soup and boil for 3 minutes after they come to the surface. Then add cucumber pieces and boil soup for 3 minutes. Makes 6 servings.

Mushroom Soup

Peking Egg Drop Soup

¼ pound lean pork shoulder, cut into fine strips
2 ounces bamboo shoots, finely sliced
4 or 5 dried black Chinese mushrooms, soaked 30 minutes in warm water and cut into small pieces
2 tablespoons vinegar
2 teaspoons soy sauce
¼ teaspoon (or less) ground pepper
1 quart chicken broth
½ teaspoon salt (or salt to taste)
1½ tablespoons cornstarch in 2 tablespoons water
1 egg, beaten

Brown strips of pork well in wok. Add bamboo shoots, mushrooms, vinegar, soy sauce, pepper, chicken broth, salt, and cornstarch mixture. Bring mixture to a full boil, stirring constantly. Reduce heat.

Add egg, a small amount at a time, stirring with a fork to separate it into shreds as it coagulates. Remove from heat and serve at once. Makes 4 to 6 servings.

Green Mustard Cabbage and Dried Shrimp Soup

1 bunch green mustard cabbage (¾ pound), cut crosswise into 1½-inch pieces
½ cup large dried shrimp
4½ cups water
1 tablespoon vegetable oil
1 teaspoon salt

Keep cabbage leaf and stalk pieces separate. Wash and soak dried shrimp in 1 cup water for 1/2 hour. Drain shrimp but save liquid. Add shrimp to very hot oil and fry them for 2 or 3 minutes. Add remaining water and shrimp liquid and simmer for 1/2 hour. Add cabbage stalks and boil them for 1 minute; add the leaves and boil for 2 minutes. Serve soup immediately.

Finely sliced lean pork or beef may be substituted for the shrimp. Combine 1/2 cup meat with water or soup, add salt, and simmer for 1/2 hour. Add cabbage with stalks and leaves separated. Watercress, celery cabbage, or spinach may be substituted for mustard cabbage. Makes 6 servings.

Dumplings with Green Peppers and Bean Sprouts

Chicken Egg Drop Soup

6 cups chicken broth
2 tablespoons cornstarch in 2 tablespoons water
1 tablespoon soy sauce
½ teaspoon sugar

2 eggs, lightly beaten
Salt and pepper
2 scallions, sliced (green tops included)

Bring chicken broth to a boil. Combine cornstarch mixture with soy sauce and sugar. Slowly stir into broth. Heat and continue stirring until soup is thickened and clear. Remove from heat. Gradually add eggs, stirring with a fork until eggs separate into shreds. Season to taste with salt and pepper. Serve immediately garnished with sliced scallions. Makes 4 servings.

Noodle Soup

1 (14-ounce) box egg noodles
2 eggs
½ tablespoon vegetable oil
5 medium dried mushrooms or ½ cup canned mushrooms
½ roll salted mustard cabbage root, if desired
5 cups meat, abalone, or chicken stock
1 tablespoon salt

3 tablespoons soy sauce
2 green onions, finely chopped
2 large pieces canned abalone
½ pound roast pork

Sauce
1 tablespoon peanut or vegetable oil
¼ cup soy sauce

Cook noodles in salted boiling water for 15 minutes. Drain and set them aside. Beat eggs slightly. Heat oil in a wok. Fry eggs in one thin layer for 1 to 2 minutes or until firm. Turn over once. Fry for 1 minute. Remove from wok and allow to cool.

Soak dried mushrooms in water for 20 to 30 minutes. Drain mushrooms, remove, and discard stems. Wash salted cabbage root 3 or 4 times with cold water. Add cabbage root and mushrooms to the stock and boil slowly for 45 minutes. Add salt, soy sauce, and onions. Simmer for 2 to 3 minutes and remove mushrooms.

Cut mushrooms, abalone, roast pork, and fried eggs into narrow strips about 1-1/2 inches long and 1/8 inch wide. Place noodles in a serving bowl. Spread abalone over noodles, then add mushrooms, roast pork, and eggs. When ready to eat, pour hot soup over this.

Combine peanut oil and soy sauce and heat in a saucepan; serve sauce at the table to season soup with. Makes 8 servings.

Hot-and-Sour Soup

3 cups chicken broth	2 tablespoons soy sauce
⅓ pound lean pork, shredded into matchstick-sized pieces	2 tablespoons dry sherry
	1 teaspoon salt
4 Chinese dried black mushrooms, soaked for 20 to 30 minutes in warm water, and sliced	½ teaspoon pepper
	2 tablespoons vinegar
	1 tablespoon cornstarch in 2 tablespoons cold water
2 ounces bean curd, cut into matchstick-sized pieces	

Bring broth to a boil in the wok and add pork, mushrooms, and bean curd. Simmer for 8 minutes, until pork is done. Add soy sauce, sherry, salt, pepper, vinegar, and cornstarch mixture. Continue to heat until soup has thickened. Serve hot. Makes 4 to 6 servings.

Crispy Fried Vegetables

Oriental Soup

1 quart chicken broth	2 ounces cooked chicken, cut into thin strips
½ cup bamboo shoots, cut into thin strips	½ teaspoon salt
2 ounces whole, cooked shrimp	¼ teaspoon soy sauce
½ pound cooked lean pork, cut into thin strips	

Heat the chicken broth and add remaining ingredients. Simmer for 3 to 4 minutes or until ingredients are hot. Makes 4 to 6 servings.

Pork and Watercress Soup

½ pound lean pork, shredded	1 teaspoon salt
6 cups chicken broth	¼ teaspoon pepper
1 small onion, thinly sliced	1 cup watercress, washed, firmly packed, and cut into 1-inch pieces
1 celery stalk, thinly sliced	

Simmer pork in chicken broth for 10 minutes. Add onion, celery, salt, and pepper and simmer for 10 minutes longer. Add watercress and heat briefly. Makes 4 to 6 servings.

Spinach Soup with Pork

1½ bunches spinach (1½ pounds)	1 tablespoon vegetable oil
1 tablespoon soy sauce	1 clove garlic, mashed
2¼ teaspoons salt	6 cups boiling water
½ cup sliced lean pork, sliced 1½ × ½ × ¼ inches	

Remove tough stems from spinach and wash leafy portions thoroughly. Add soy sauce and 1/4 teaspoon salt to pork. Heat oil in a wok, add the mashed garlic and pork, and fry them for 3 minutes. Remove garlic if desired. Add boiling water and 2 teaspoons salt; simmer for 10 minutes. Add spinach and simmer for 5 minutes. Serve hot.

One-fourth cup dried shrimp may be substituted for pork and the salt reduced to 1-1/2 teaspoons. Wash and soak shrimp for 15 minutes. Drain, but keep the liquid. Fry shrimp, add liquid, and simmer for 10 minutes; then add spinach. Makes 6 servings.

Vegetable Curry

Fried Rice with Chicken and Ham

Mushroom Soup

3 cups chicken stock or water and 2 chicken stock cubes
½-inch slice root ginger or ¼ teaspoon ground ginger
2 spring onions, thinly sliced
¼ pound button mushrooms, thinly sliced
Salt and pepper

Place stock, ginger, and spring onions in a wok. Bring to a boil, then cover pan and simmer for 20 minutes. Add mushrooms and simmer for a further 10 minutes. Add salt and pepper to taste. Remove ginger and serve piping hot. Makes 4 servings.

Watercress Soup

4 cups watercress, cut in 2-inch pieces
4½ cups water
1 teaspoon salt
¼ cup fresh lean pork, sliced 1½ × ½ × ¼ inches

Wash watercress thoroughly and discard tough stems. Cut watercress and keep tougher portions separate. Combine water, salt, and pork and simmer for 30 minutes. Add tough watercress and boil for 1 minute. Add watercress tips, boil for 1 minute, and serve immediately. Makes 5 servings.

Vegetables and Rice

Stir-Fry Broccoli with Shoyu Ginger Sauce

1 head fresh broccoli or 1 package frozen, defrosted broccoli	½ tablespoon soy sauce
	⅛ teaspoon powdered ginger
	½ cup chicken broth
2 tablespoons vegetable oil	½ teaspoon salt

Sauce
½ tablespoon cornstarch

Prepare fresh broccoli for stir-frying by breaking off branches from the main stem and slicing branch stems very thin. Cut each floret into several bite-sized pieces. Heat oil in wok and add broccoli. Stir-fry for 1 minute; cover and steam for 3 minutes. Broccoli should still be bright green in color—crisp, but heated through.

Serve at once with ginger sauce, which has been prepared by combining the sauce ingredients and bringing them to a boil, stirring constantly. Sauce may be served separately or poured over broccoli just before the broccoli is removed from the wok. Makes 4 servings.

Stir-Fried Bean Sprouts

1 tablespoon vegetable oil	1 tablespoon soy sauce
2 cups bean sprouts	

Heat oil in wok and stir-fry sprouts for 1 to 2 minutes, or until heated through but still crisp. Serve at once sprinkled with a little soy sauce. Makes 4 servings.

Chinese Mushrooms and Bamboo Shoots with Hoisin Sauce

2 tablespoons vegetable oil	½ teaspoon salt
½ pound fresh mushrooms, cut into "T" shapes	1 teaspoon cornstarch in 1 tablespoon cold water
4 ounces bamboo shoots, sliced (½ small can)	2 tablespoons hoisin sauce

Heat oil in wok. Stir-fry mushrooms for 2 to 3 minutes; add bamboo shoots and stir-fry 1 minute longer. Combine remaining ingredients and add to vegetables. Heat and stir gently until sauce thickens and vegetables are coated. Serve at once. Makes 4 servings.

Sweet-and-Sour Carrots

2 tablespoons vegetable oil	1 tablespoon vinegar
1 slice fresh gingerroot	½ tablespoon brown sugar
1 pound carrots, cleaned and roll-cut into 1-inch pieces	2 teaspoons cornstarch in 2 tablespoons cold water
½ teaspoon salt	½ cup canned pineapple chunks (optional)
½ cup chicken broth	

Heat oil in wok. Brown and discard ginger slice. Stir-fry carrots for 1 minute. Add salt and chicken broth. Cover and steam over moderate heat for 5 minutes. Stir in vinegar, brown sugar, cornstarch mixture, and pineapple chunks (if desired). Heat until sauce thickens. Serve at once. Makes 4 servings.

Fried Rice Sub Gum

Celery and Mushrooms

2 tablespoons vegetable oil	1 teaspoon sugar
½ pound mushrooms, cut into "T" shapes	2 teaspoons soy sauce
1 small bunch celery, sliced diagonally into ½-inch slices	

Heat oil in wok and stir-fry mushrooms 1 minute. Add celery, sugar, and soy sauce. Stir-fry 2 to 3 minutes, or just until celery becomes a brighter green. Serve at once. Makes 4 servings.

Stir-Fried Chinese Celery Cabbage

2 tablespoons vegetable oil	½ teaspoon salt
1 slice fresh gingerroot	½ teaspoon sugar
1 pound Chinese celery cabbage (bok choy), cut diagonally into ¼-inch slices	3 tablespoons chicken broth
	1 teaspoon sesame oil
3 stalks celery, cut diagonally into ¼-inch slices	

Heat oil in wok. Brown and discard ginger slice. Stir-fry bok choy and celery for 2 to 3 minutes. Add salt, sugar, and chicken broth. Cover and heat for 1 minute. Serve at once sprinkled with a little sesame oil. Makes 4 servings.

Dumplings with Green Peppers and Bean Sprouts

Basic Dumpling Dough
1 cup flour, sifted
1 egg
Dash salt
1½ tablespoons cold water

Filling
1 green onion, finely chopped
1 clove garlic, chopped
1 cup cabbage, finely chopped
Salt
Dash pepper
¼ pound Oriental green peppers
2 cups bean sprouts
2 tablespoons sesame oil

Mix flour and salt. Stir in egg, then water, until a stiff mixture is formed. Roll out to thin, flat dough with a rolling pin on a floured surface. Cut into approximately 2-inch circles with sharp knife or cookie cutter.

Make filling: Stir-fry filling ingredients in wok, into which 1 tablespoon sesame oil has been heated. Lightly stir-fry filling mixture until sizzling nicely and starting to brown, about 4 to 5 minutes. Remove; place into bowl and let cool for several minutes.

Fill each dough circle with about 1 teaspoon of filling; fold over in half and seal together 2 curved open edges by crimping with your fingertips. Boil in salted water for 4 minutes. Drain; add to wok into which 2 tablespoons sesame oil has been heated. Add the green peppers, then the bean sprouts, and stir-fry over medium heat for about 5 minutes. Serve immediately. Makes 4 servings.

Stir-Fried Green Beans

2	tablespoons vegetable oil	½	cup chicken broth
1	clove garlic	½	teaspoon salt
2 to 3	cups green beans, washed, stemmed, and cut into 1-inch pieces	½	teaspoon sugar
		1	teaspoon cornstarch in 1 tablespoon cold water

Heat oil in wok. Brown and discard garlic. Stir-fry green beans for 3 minutes; add chicken broth, salt, and sugar. Cover and steam over moderate heat for 3 to 4 minutes, until beans are tender but still bright green and crisp.

Stir cornstarch mixture and add it to wok. Cook, stirring, until sauce is thickened. Serve at once. Makes 4 servings.

Crispy Fried Vegetables

1 cup all-purpose flour, sifted	2 potatoes
1 egg	1 stick celery
½ cup milk	8 small cauliflower florets
Salt and pepper	1 sliced onion
2 carrots	2 cups oil for frying

Prepare batter by combining flour, egg, milk, and a little salt and pepper in a small bowl. Mix or whisk until batter is smooth and lump-free. Batter should be thin; if it seems very thick, add more milk.

Cut the vegetables into matchstick-sized strips. Thoroughly mix vegetables into batter. Let stand for 1/2 hour. Using a slotted spoon, lift out spoonfuls of mixed vegetables and drop gently into deep fat at 375°F. (Use an electric wok or a thermometer to maintain proper temperature of the fat.) Deep-fry for 2 to 3 minutes, a few spoonfuls at a time. Lift out and drain on paper towels. Makes 4 to 6 servings.

Vegetable Curry

1 tablespoon oil	1 small turnip
2 large onions, coarsely chopped	2 potatoes
2 cloves garlic, crushed	1 cup green beans
1 level teaspoon chili powder or to taste	1 pound can tomatoes
2 to 3 level tablespoons curry powder	Sea salt
	1 cooking apple
4 carrots	¼ cup raisins
	1 cup brown rice

Heat oil in wok. Add onion and garlic and stir-fry gently for 5 minutes. Stir in chili powder and curry powder and cook for 1 minute. Cut carrots, turnip, potatoes, and green beans into 1-inch pieces. Add these vegetables to wok and stir to coat them with curry mixture. Add can of tomatoes and salt to taste. Cover and simmer for 30 minutes, stirring occasionally.

Peel, core, and cut apple into 1/2-inch cubes. Gently stir apple cubes and raisins into curry, taking care not to break up the cooked vegetables. Cook, uncovered, for a further 10 minutes.

Meanwhile, cook brown rice in boiling salted water for about 50 minutes or until cooked. Arrange rice round the edge of a serving dish and pour the curry into the middle. Serve with a selection of side salads, for example: sliced banana, melon cubes, tomato, and onion salad. Cashews, peanuts and chutney are also good curry accompaniments. Makes 4 servings.

Deep-Fried Beef with Scallions

Tossed Spinach with Peanuts

1 **pound fresh spinach, washed and stemmed**	1 **tablespoon vegetable oil**
¼ **cup peanuts (or more)**	1 **tablespoon soy sauce**
	Salt and pepper

Steam spinach in a small amount of boiling water for only 2 to 3 minutes. Drain at once, pat dry, and cut into fine strips. Crush 1/2 the peanuts with a rolling pin or mince with a cleaver.

Heat oil in wok and add crushed peanuts, spinach, soy sauce, and salt and pepper to taste. Stir-fry for 1 to 2 minutes. Serve garnished with remaining peanuts. Makes 4 servings.

Five Precious Oriental Vegetables

5 to 6 Chinese dried black mushrooms	2 tablespoons vegetable oil
1 small head of Chinese celery cabbage	1 cup bean sprouts
	3 tablespoons chicken broth
1 or 2 bamboo shoots	1 teaspoon salt
4 or 5 water chestnuts	2 teaspoons soy sauce
	1 teaspoon sugar

Soak mushrooms in warm water for 20 to 30 minutes; drain, remove and discard the tough stems and cut the caps into strips. Wash cabbage well; drain and cut diagonally into 1/2-inch slices. Cut bamboo shoots and water chestnuts into slices.

Heat oil in wok. Stir-fry cabbage 1 minute, then add mushrooms, bean sprouts, water chestnuts, and bamboo shoots. Stir-fry all together for 3 to 4 minutes. Add broth with the remaining ingredients. Mix well and heat through. Vegetables should be tender but still crisp. Serve at once. Makes 4 servings.

Mixed Vegetables Chinese-Style

2 tablespoons vegetable oil	½ pound bok choy or white cabbage, cut into ¼-inch slices
1 green pepper, cut into ¼-inch strips	
1 medium onion, cut into ¼-inch slices	Toasted sesame seeds
3 stalks celery, cut diagonally into ¼-inch slices	

Heat oil in wok. Add all the vegetables and stir-fry for 4 to 5 minutes or until they are heated. Serve at once sprinkled with sesame seeds. (You may also steam vegetables in a small amount of water in the covered wok for 4 to 5 minutes.) Makes 4 servings.

Sweet-and-Sour Vegetable Medley

2   tablespoons vegetable oil
2   medium potatoes, peeled
     and very thinly sliced
2   medium carrots, very
     thinly sliced diagonally
4   scallions, sliced
1   cup green beans
½   cucumber, unpeeled and
     sliced into ⅛-inch slices

Sauce
1   tablespoon cornstarch
1   tablespoon soy sauce
1   tablespoon vinegar
1   tablespoon tomato paste
1   tablespoon dry sherry
2   teaspoons sugar

Heat oil in wok and stir-fry potatoes 1 minute. Add carrots; stir-fry 1 minute. Add scallions and green beans and continue to stir-fry until vegetables are heated through.

Stir ingredients for the sauce together and add to vegetables in the wok. Add cucumber slices and gently stir vegetables and sauce until sauce thickens and cucumbers are heated. Serve at once. Makes 4 servings.

Fried Rice with Chicken and Ham

3   tablespoons vegetable oil
4   ounces cooked chicken,
     finely chopped
4   ounces cooked ham, finely
     chopped
2   scallions, sliced
2 to 3 cups cold, boiled rice
     (prepared a day ahead and
     chilled)

1   tablespoon soy sauce
¼   teaspoon salt
1 to 2 eggs, beaten
2   tablespoons cooked peas
1-egg omelet (optional
     garnish)

Heat oil in wok; stir-fry chicken and ham 1 to 2 minutes. Add scallions and rice; continue to stir-fry until rice is hot and golden in color. Add soy sauce and salt.

Make a well in rice; pour in beaten eggs. Stir and heat until eggs have coagulated. Add peas; heat for 1 minute longer. Garnish with 1-egg omelet cut into 1/4-inch strips. Makes 4 to 6 servings.

Shredded Beef with Vegetables

Fried Rice with Ham

3	tablespoons vegetable oil	3	ounces cooked ham, cut into small strips
1	medium onion, chopped		
2	stalks celery, cut into ¼-inch slices	2	eggs, beaten with salt and pepper
2	cups cold, boiled rice		

Heat oil in wok and stir-fry onion and celery 3 to 4 minutes, until they are translucent. Add rice and ham and stir-fry together 4 to 5 minutes, until rice is golden. Pour eggs into a well in the rice. Heat and stir until all egg has coagulated. Serve at once. Makes 4 to 6 servings.

Fried Rice Sub Gum

3 tablespoons vegetable oil	4 ounces cooked small
1 medium onion, chopped	shrimp, left whole
1 green pepper, thinly sliced	3 to 4 cups cold, cooked rice
4 ounces cooked ham, diced	1 to 2 tablespoons soy sauce
into ¼-inch pieces	2-egg omelet (optional
4 ounces cooked chicken,	garnish)
diced into ¼-inch pieces	

Heat oil in wok and stir-fry onion until it is translucent. Push aside. Stir-fry green pepper for 1 to 2 minutes. Return onions to wok. Add meat, shrimp, and rice and stir-fry together for 4 to 5 minutes, until rice is golden. Sprinkle with soy sauce and garnish with 1/8-inch strips of omelette. Makes 6 to 8 servings.

Vegetable and Ham Rice Cake

2 tablespoons vinegar	½ unpeeled cucumber, sliced
2 tablespoons sugar	3 scallions, sliced
½ teaspoon salt	2 tablespoons soy sauce
3 cups cooked, cold rice	2 teaspoons prepared
2 tablespoons vegetable oil	horseradish sauce
3 carrots, cut into	2 tablespoons light cream
matchstick-sized pieces	4 slices boiled ham,
2 ounces mushrooms, sliced	shredded

Combine vinegar, 1 tablespoon of the sugar, and salt together with the rice. Toss well. Heat oil in wok. Add carrots and stir-fry 2 to 3 minutes. Add mushrooms, cucumber, and scallions and continue to stir-fry until all vegetables are very tender. Stir in remaining 1 tablespoon of sugar and soy sauce. Set aside.

Grease an 8-inch springform pan (or use an 8-inch square baking pan lined with plastic wrap extending well over the sides so the mixture can eventually be lifted out). Pack 1/2 of the rice in the bottom. Cover with 3/4 of the prepared vegetables, then the remaining rice. Combine horseradish sauce and cream and spread over rice. Cover with remaining 1/4 of the vegetables and the ham shreds. Place a piece of waxed paper over the top and weight it down. Chill for 30 minutes. Remove weight and paper, then carefully remove cake from pan. Use a wet knife to cut cake into slices and arrange on a platter. Serve cold with a little soy sauce. Makes 4 servings.

Shrimp and Egg Fried Rice

1 **slice bacon**	2 **cups cold, cooked rice**
2 **scallions, sliced**	1 **egg beaten with salt and**
1 **clove garlic, minced**	**pepper**
3 **ounces shrimp, cut into**	1 to 2 tablespoons soy sauce
small pieces	

Fry bacon in wok until crisp; remove and set aside. Add scallions and garlic to wok and stir-fry in bacon fat for 1 to 2 minutes. Add shrimp and stir-fry until pink (if frozen or canned shrimp are used, add while stir-frying rice). Add rice and stir-fry 4 to 5 minutes, until rice is golden. Pour beaten egg into a well in the rice. Stir and heat until egg has coagulated. Crumble bacon and add to rice with the soy sauce. Combine well. Makes 4 to 6 servings.

Beef Shreds with Carrots and Green Pepper

Meats

Beef with Bamboo Shoots and Peppers

1 **pound beef (round or flank), cut into thin strips**	1 **red pepper (a green one that has vine-ripened), if available, cut into ½-inch slices**
2 **tablespoons soy sauce**	
2 **tablespoons dry sherry**	
1 **tablespoon cornstarch**	2 **scallions, cut into ½-inch slices**
½ **teaspoon sugar**	
1 **clove garlic, halved**	1 **(8-ounce) can bamboo shoots, sliced**
2 **tablespoons vegetable oil**	
1 **green pepper, cut into ½-inch strips**	½ **cup chicken or beef broth**

Marinate beef strips in combined soy sauce, sherry, cornstarch, and sugar for 20 to 30 minutes. Brown garlic in vegetable oil. Remove and discard garlic. Stir-fry pepper strips 2 to 3 minutes; push up the sides. Stir-fry scallions and bamboo shoots 1 to 2 minutes; push up the sides. Stir-fry beef 3 to 4 minutes.

Return vegetables to the beef in the wok and add broth. Stir and heat until sauce boils. Serve at once with rice. Makes 4 servings.

Beef with Asparagus and Hoisin Sauce

1 tablespoon soy sauce
1 tablespoon dry sherry
1 teaspoon cornstarch
1 teaspoon garlic, grated
1 pound flank steak, thinly sliced with the knife held at 45° angle to the board
2 tablespoons vegetable oil
2 scallions, cut into ¼-inch diagonal slices
1 pound asparagus, cut diagonally into ¼-inch slices
3 tablespoons hoisin sauce
½ cup roasted peanuts

Combine soy sauce, dry sherry, cornstarch, and grated garlic. Add beef and marinate it for 20 to 30 minutes. Heat oil in wok and stir-fry scallions for 1 to 2 minutes; push aside. Stir-fry asparagus for 2 to 3 minutes; push aside. Stir-fry beef 3 to 4 minutes, until done. Return the vegetables to the beef. Stir in hoisin sauce and peanuts and serve at once. Makes 4 servings.

Steak Chinese

Burmese Ginger Beef

1	cup onions, minced	3	pounds lean stew beef
2	cloves garlic, pressed	½	cup peanut oil
1	teaspoon chili powder	8	medium fresh tomatoes,
2	teaspoons turmeric		peeled and cut into large
2	teaspoons ginger		pieces
1	teaspoon salt	4	cups beef stock

Combine onions, garlic, chili powder, turmeric, ginger, and salt in a bowl, mixing well. Cut beef into 1-1/2-inch cubes and place in a shallow nonmetal dish. Sprinkle with onion mixture, then refrigerate for 3 hours, stirring occasionally.

Heat oil in wok. Add beef and stir-fry, until browned on all sides. Place beef in a casserole and add skillet drippings, tomatoes, and beef stock. Bake, covered, in a preheated 325°F oven for about 2 hours or until the beef is tender. Serve with boiled rice and garnish with red sweet pepper strips. Makes about 6 to 8 servings.

Chinese Beef

½	cup dried Chinese mushrooms	¼	teaspoon ginger
		3	tablespoons soy sauce
1½	pounds flank steak	2	tablespoons sherry
2	small tomatoes, peeled	½	teaspoon sugar
1	green pepper	1	(1-pound) can bean
2	tablespoons olive oil		sprouts, drained
1	clove garlic, crushed	1	tablespoon cornstarch
1	teaspoon salt	3	tablespoons water
Dash pepper			

Soak Chinese mushrooms in water to cover for 20 minutes. Drain and halve large mushrooms. Cut flank steaks in strips across grain (about 2 x 1 x 1/4 inches). Cut tomatoes in eighths. Cut green pepper in 1-inch cubes.

Heat oil in wok. Add flank steak strips, garlic, salt, pepper, and ginger. Sauté over high heat until meat is evenly browned on all sides. Add soy sauce, sherry, sugar, tomatoes, green pepper, mushrooms, and bean sprouts. Stir until well mixed, cover, and cook over medium heat for 5 minutes.

Make a paste of the cornstarch and water and add to beef mixture. Cook, uncovered, stirring occasionally, until sauce thickens. Makes 4 to 6 servings.

Note: Tomatoes can be peeled easily by dipping in boiling water for a few seconds or by holding directly over a flame for a few seconds. (If the second method is used, be sure fork used to hold tomato has a wooden handle.)

Calves Liver with Bean Sprouts

Beef with Oyster Sauce

2	tablespoons soy sauce	2	tablespoons vegetable oil
1	tablespoon dry sherry	1	green pepper, cut into ¼-inch strips
1	tablespoon cornstarch		
1	teaspoon sugar	8	canned water chestnuts, sliced
1	pound beef (chuck or round), cut into ¼-inch strips	2½	tablespoons bottled oyster sauce

Combine soy sauce, dry sherry, cornstarch, and sugar in a small bowl. Add beef and marinate 20 to 30 minutes. Heat oil in wok and stir-fry green pepper strips and water chestnuts 1 to 2 minutes. Push aside and stir-fry beef 2 to 3 minutes. Return green pepper and water chestnuts to beef in wok. Gently stir in oyster sauce. Heat through and serve at once garnished with nuts, if desired. Makes 4 servings.

Deep-Fried Beef with Scallions

1   pound beef (flank or
    round) cut into ¼- x 3-
    inch strips

Frying Batter
1   large egg
1   cup all-purpose flour,
    sifted
¾   cup water
2   cups oil for frying
8   scallions, sliced into ½-
    inch slices

1   clove garlic, minced
1   teaspoon ginger root,
    grated
2   tablespoons vegetable oil
½   teaspoon salt
¼   cup dry white wine
1 to 2 tablespoons soy sauce
2   tablespoons black bean
    sauce

Combine batter ingredients. Let stand for 1 hour. Dip beef strips, a few at a time, into batter and deep-fry in oil at 400°F. Drain on paper towels and keep warm.

Combine remaining ingredients and simmer, covered, for 20 minutes. Place scallion mixture on a serving platter and top with deep-fried beef. Serve with boiled rice. Makes 4 servings.

Foil-Wrapped Beef

1   pound beef (top of the
    round or chuck blade
    steak or roast), very thinly
    sliced (partial freezing may
    make this step easier)
2   tablespoons hoisin sauce
1   tablespoon soy sauce

1   tablespoon dry sherry
1   tablespoon cornstarch
4   (12-inch) aluminum foil
    squares
1   scallion, finely sliced
Parsley leaves

Combine beef, hoisin sauce, soy sauce, dry sherry, and cornstarch. Place 1/4 of this mixture in a single layer in the center of each foil square. Top each with sliced scallion and parsley leaves. (You can divide mixture into smaller portions and make 6 to 8 squares.)

Fold into flat packages about 5 inches square. Keeping seams up to prevent the escape of juices, bake at 450°F for 6 minutes. Serve still wrapped so the diner can release the flavorful juices at the moment of eating. (It is important to wrap in a single layer in a flat package or the beef will not be uniformly cooked.) Makes 4 servings.

Beef Fuji

2 tablespoons vegetable oil
1 pound beef steak (round, chuck blade, or flank steak), 1 to 1½ inches thick, cut into thin strips
½ pound fresh mushrooms, sliced into "T" shapes
1 small onion, sliced
½ cup chicken or beef broth
¼ cup soy sauce
1 tablespoon cornstarch in 2 tablespoons cold water
1 (8-ounce) can bamboo shoots, sliced
1 (8-ounce) can water chestnuts, sliced
3 scallions, cut into 1-inch lengths
1 (6-ounce) package frozen, defrosted pea pods
1 (1-pound) can sliced peaches, drained

Heat oil in wok and stir-fry beef, mushrooms, and onion for 4 to 5 minutes. Add broth, soy sauce, and cornstarch mixture. Cook, stirring constantly, until sauce thickens. Add vegetables and peaches. Continue heating until vegetables are heated through. Serve at once with rice. Makes 4 servings.

Chinese-Style Lamb

Red-Stewed Beef Tongue

1 beef tongue	2 tablespoons dark soy sauce per pound of meat
Boiling water to cover meat	
½ clove garlic	1 teaspoon sugar per pound of meat
1 tablespoon oil	
2 tablespoons cooking wine	

Immerse tongue completely in boiling water, turn off heat, and let soak 1 minute. Remove tongue from water and use a blunt knife to peel off skin.

Brown garlic in oil in a wok, then brown tongue on both sides. Lower heat and add cooking wine. For each pound of tongue, add 2 tablespoons dark soy sauce. Cook over low heat for 1-1/2 to 2 hours. Turn tongue at 20-minute intervals. Add water to maintain quantity of cooking liquid at 6 to 8 tablespoons. During last 20 minutes, add 1 teaspoon of sugar per pound and serve. Makes about 4 servings.

Sate Beef

1 pound sirloin steak	3 teaspoons bottled sate sauce
1½ teaspoons soy sauce	
¼ teaspoon pepper	1 teaspoon dry sherry
1 teaspoon sesame oil	½ teaspoon sugar
1 teaspoon cornstarch	1 teaspoon curry powder
1 tablespoon water	1 teaspoon salt
2 tablespoons oil	1 tablespoon water
1 clove garlic, crushed	1 teaspoon soy sauce
1 medium onion, diced	

Trim all fat from meat; cut into 1/4-inch slices. Gently pound each slice to flatten slightly. Put meat into bowl with 1-1/2 teaspoons soy sauce, pepper, sesame oil, cornstarch, and 1 tablespoon water. Mix well; allow to stand at least 20 minutes.

Heat oil in wok. Sauté meat until brown on both sides. Remove from pan; keep warm. Add garlic and peeled and diced onion to wok; sauté gently until onion is transparent.

Combine sate sauce, sherry, sugar, curry powder, salt, 1 tablespoon water, and 1 teaspoon soy sauce. Add this to onions in wok; stir until boiling.

Return beef to wok; cook until beef is tender, about 1 minute. Put in warmed serving dish. Makes 2 to 4 servings.

Almond-Sprinkled Pork Stew

Red-Stewed Shin of Beef

2	tablespoons cooking oil	1	teaspoon salt
2	pounds shin of beef	2	teaspoons sugar
⅛	teaspoon pepper	¼	cup soy sauce
2	slices fresh gingerroot	1	teaspoon sesame seed oil
1	clove garlic	1	teaspoon sherry
1	scallion, halved		Water to cover the meat

Heat oil in wok; when it is hot, add meat and brown on both sides. Add pepper, gingerroot, garlic, and scallion. Add salt and sugar and pour soy sauce, sesame seed oil, and sherry over it. Add enough boiling water to cover meat. Bring liquid to a boil, cover, and turn down heat. Simmer slowly for 2-1/2 hours.

Remove meat and cut into slices 1/4 inch thick; arrange on a shallow dish. Pour gravy over it and serve at once. Makes about 4 servings.

Shredded Beef with Vegetables

1	pound beef (round or flank steak), sliced very thin and cut into strips 2 inches long	1	carrot, cut into very fine 2-inch shreds
1	teaspoon sugar	1	onion, sliced into ¼-inch slices
1	tablespoon soy sauce	1	cup bean sprouts
¼	teaspoon salt	1	tablespoon cornstarch in ½ cup chicken stock or water
2	tablespoons vegetable oil	1	tablespoon dry sherry

Marinate beef strips for 10 to 20 minutes in the combined sugar, soy sauce, and salt. Heat oil in wok and stir-fry carrot shreds and onion rings 2 to 3 minutes; push aside. Stir-fry bean sprouts 1 to 2 minutes; push aside. Stir-fry strips of beef 2 to 3 minutes. Return vegetables to beef in wok.

Combine cornstarch mixture and dry sherry. Add to beef and vegetables; heat and stir until sauce is thickened. Serve at once with fried rice. Makes 4 servings.

Beef Shreds with Carrots and Green Pepper

2	tablespoons vegetable oil	1½	cups bean sprouts
2	thin slices of gingerroot	1	pound cooked beef, thinly sliced
1	clove garlic, halved		
1	large green pepper, cut into thin strips	2	tablespoons soy sauce
2	carrots, shredded	1	tablespoon cornstarch in ½ cup chicken broth or water
1	onion, sliced		

Heat oil in wok and brown ginger slices and garlic clove. Remove and discard ginger and garlic. Stir-fry green pepper and carrots 2 to 3 minutes; push aside. Stir-fry onion 1 to 2 minutes; push aside. Stir-fry bean sprouts 1 minute; push aside. Stir-fry beef strips until heated. Return vegetables to beef in wok.

Stir soy sauce into cornstarch mixture and add to wok. Heat until sauce boils and thickens and ingredients are heated through. Serve on a bed of boiled rice with shrimp crackers. Makes 4 servings.

Beef with Snow Pea Pods and Mushrooms

2 tablespoons vegetable oil	1 pound flank steak, cut into thin slices
1 teaspoon fresh gingerroot, grated	½ cup chicken broth or water
1 clove garlic, grated	1 tablespoon cornstarch in 2 tablespoons water
½ pound mushrooms, sliced into "T" shapes	3 tablespoons soy sauce
14 to 16 snow pea pods, strings removed	¼ cup cashews or peanuts

Heat oil in wok and stir-fry ginger, garlic, and mushrooms 1 to 2 minutes; push aside. Stir-fry pea pods 1 to 2 minutes; or until they become bright green; push aside. Stir-fry beef 2 to 3 minutes. Return vegetables to meat. Add broth, cornstarch mixture, and soy sauce and heat until sauce boils and is thickened, and beef and vegetables are heated through.

Add nuts and serve at once with rice. Makes 4 servings.

Javanese Spiced Pork

Beef with Snow Pea Pods and Water Chestnuts

1 tablespoon soy sauce	6 to 8 water chestnuts, sliced
1 tablespoon dry sherry	½ cup chicken broth or stock
1 pound beef (top of the round), sliced very thin	1 tablespoon soy sauce
2 tablespoons vegetable oil	1 tablespoon dry sherry
12 to 16 snow pea pods, strings removed	1 tablespoon cornstarch in 2 tablespoons cold water
	Walnuts (optional)

Combine 1 tablespoon soy sauce and 1 tablespoon dry sherry in a small bowl. Add sliced beef and let stand 20 to 30 minutes. Heat oil in wok and stir-fry pea pods 1 to 2 minutes or just until their green color brightens; push aside. Stir-fry water chestnuts 1 minute; push aside. Stir-fry beef 3 to 4 minutes. Return pea pods and water chestnuts to beef in wok.

Add broth, remaining 1 tablespoon soy sauce, remaining 1 tablespoon dry sherry, and cornstarch mixture. Heat until sauce boils and is thickened and clear. Garnish with walnuts if you wish. Serve at once with rice. Makes 4 servings.

Steak Chinese

1 pound boneless sirloin steak	1 teaspoon oyster sauce
½ teaspoon bicarbonate of soda	2 teaspoons brandy or dry sherry
1 teaspoon sugar	1 tablespoon oil
Pinch of salt	2 medium onions, sliced
1 teaspoon cornstarch	1 tablespoon brandy or dry sherry
2 teaspoons soy sauce	

Trim fat from meat; slice into 1/4-inch slices. Gently flatten with meat mallet or rolling pin. Put meat in bowl. Add soda, sugar, salt, cornstarch, soy sauce, oyster sauce, and 2 teaspoons brandy or sherry. Mix well. Cover; marinate at least 3 hours.

Heat oil in wok . Sauté onions until just golden, then transfer to heated serving plate. Add meat slices to wok gradually, spreading them out. When browned on one side, turn to brown other side. Cook quickly, only until meat is tender. Overcooking will toughen meat. Add 1 tablespoon brandy or sherry; mix well.

Arrange meat over onions; serve at once. Makes 2 to 4 servings.

Oriental Pork Loin

Beef with Snow Pea Pods and Cashews

1 **pound beef (top of the round steak), sliced into ¼-inch strips**	12 to 16 **snow pea pods, strings removed**
2 **tablespoons black bean sauce**	1 **tablespoon cornstarch in ½ cup cold broth or water**
2 **tablespoons soy sauce**	½ **cup cashews**
1 **clove garlic, grated**	1 **cup bean sprouts (if desired)**
2 **tablespoons vegetable oil**	

Marinate beef in a combined mixture of bean sauce, soy sauce, and grated garlic in a small bowl for 20 to 30 minutes. Heat oil in wok and stir-fry snow pea pods 1 to 2 minutes, until their green color brightens; push aside. Stir-fry beef 2 to 3 minutes. Return snow pea pods to beef in the wok and stir in cornstarch and broth mixture. Heat until sauce boils and is clear. Add cashews and serve at once. (Bean sprouts may be added just before cornstarch mixture is added, if desired.) Makes 4 servings.

Wok Surprise

Oil for cooking	2 **cups fresh bean sprouts**
1 **cup green pepper, sliced**	2 **cups fresh spinach, torn into bite-sized pieces**
1 **cup celery, sliced diagonally**	**Freshly ground black pepper to taste**
1 **cup zucchini, sliced**	**Soy sauce to taste**
2 **cups leftover cooked roast beef, thinly sliced**	**Cornstarch mixed with cold water**
Beef gravy, beef broth, or chicken broth	
½ **cup fresh mushrooms, sliced**	

Put small amount of oil in wok and heat to medium-high. Add green pepper and celery. Stir-fry for 1 minute. Add zucchini and stir-fry for 2 more minutes, or until the vegetables are bright in color and still crisp. Push vegetables up sides of wok (or remove) and place roast beef and a little gravy, beef broth, or chicken broth in wok; toss meat until hot.

Push meat up sides of wok; place mushrooms and bean sprouts in wok and stir-fry for 1 minute. Add previously cooked vegetables, beef, spinach, pepper, and soy sauce. If desired, you may add a little cornstarch mixed with cold water to thicken the gravy. Serve with rice, if desired. Makes 4 servings.

Oriental Pork Stew

Szechwan Beef

2 tablespoons vegetable oil
1 or 2 green peppers, cut into ⅛-inch strips
1 or 2 carrots, finely shredded into ⅛-inch matchstick-sized strips (slice lengthwise, stack slices, slice lengthwise through stack)
1 scallion, quartered lengthwise, then into 3-inch-long strips

1 pound beef (round or chuck), cut into fine slivers or strips, ⅛-inch by 2 to 3 inches long
2 tablespoons dry sherry
2 tablespoons hoisin sauce
1 tablespoon black bean sauce
1 tablespoon vinegar
1 teaspoon sugar
¼ to ½ teaspoon chili paste (very hot!)

Heat oil in wok and stir-fry green peppers, carrots, and scallion for 1 to 2 minutes; push aside. Stir-fry slivers of beef for 1 to 2 minutes and add to vegetables. Add remaining ingredients; stir and heat thoroughly. Serve at once with boiled rice. Makes 4 servings.

Calves Liver with Bean Sprouts

3 tablespoons dry sherry
1 teaspoon gingerroot, grated
1 pound calves liver, cubed into bite-sized pieces
2 tablespoons vegetable oil
¼ cup blanched, whole almonds
2 medium onions, finely chopped

¼ pound mushrooms, cut into cubes
1 cup fresh or frozen, defrosted peas
½ cup chicken or beef broth
2 tablespoons soy sauce
1 cup bean sprouts
1 tablespoon cornstarch in 2 tablespoons cold water

Combine sherry and grated ginger in small bowl and add cubed liver. Marinate for 20 to 30 minutes. Heat oil in wok and stir-fry almonds for 2 to 3 minutes, until browned. Remove from pan. Stir-fry onions with mushrooms 2 to 3 minutes. More oil may be necessary. Push aside. Stir-fry peas 1 to 3 minutes; push aside. Stir-fry liver 2 to 3 minutes. Return vegetables and almonds to the wok.

Add broth, soy sauce, and bean sprouts. Stir in cornstarch mixture and heat until sauce becomes thick and clear and bean sprouts are heated through. Serve at once with rice. Makes 4 servings.

Chinese-Style Lamb

1 (2-pound) boneless leg of lamb
Salt and pepper
2 tablespoons vegetable oil
1 small onion, sliced
2 large carrots, sliced
1 tablespoon corn syrup
3 tablespoons tomato catsup

1 tablespoon soy sauce or Worcestershire sauce
1 tablespoon juice from pineapple rings
1 (8-ounce) can pineapple rings
1 bunch spring onions

Remove and discard excess fat from meat. Cut meat into 1-inch cubes. Season well with salt and pepper.

Heat oil in a wok. Gently fry lamb, onion, and sliced carrots until golden. Add syrup, catsup, soy or Worcestershire sauce, and 1 tablespoon of juice from pineapple rings.

Drain pineapple rings and cut them in half. Wash spring onions and cut off some of the green part.

Cover pan with tightly fitting lid and simmer very gently for 45 minutes or until lamb is very tender. Add pineapple and spring onions about 5 minutes before end of cooking time. Serve with boiled rice, mixed with peas, and, if you like, bean sprouts. Makes about 4 servings.

Almond-Sprinkled Pork Stew

1 pound sliced pork shoulder	2 onions
½ teaspoon paprika powder	1 green and 1 red paprika
1 teaspoon curry	1 cup celery root, grated
2 tablespoons flour	1 grated apple (not sweet)
2 cups bouillon	½ cup almonds
	Soy sauce

Cut pork in fine strips and brown slightly in a wok. Turn over to casserole. Sprinkle paprika powder, curry, and flour over the pork and hot bouillon while stirring briskly. Brown small wedges of onion, strips of paprika, celery, and apple in the wok and add to pork. Simmer tightly covered for about 25 minutes. Add liquid, if necessary, and season to taste.

Halve the almonds and brown slightly in wok in a small amount of oil. Serve with soy sauce over rice. Makes about 4 servings.

Pork with Peppers and Cashews

Curried Pork with Shrimp

½ pound pork (shoulder or butt), shredded into thin strips
2 tablespoons soy sauce
2 tablespoons vegetable oil
2 teaspoons curry powder
1 small onion, minced
3 celery stalks, cut into ¼-inch slices

2 scallions, cut into ⅛-inch slices
½ tablespoon cornstarch in ½ cup water or chicken broth
½ pound whole cooked shrimp

Marinate pork in soy sauce for 20 minutes. Heat oil in wok and brown curry powder and onion until aroma becomes strong. Stir-fry pork for about 4 minutes or until well done; push aside.

Combine celery and scallions and stir-fry 1 to 2 minutes. Return pork and add cornstarch mixture. Heat until sauce is clear and thickened and shrimp are heated through. Serve with noodles. Makes 4 servings.

Javanese Spiced Pork

1½ pounds boneless pork, thinly sliced
2 large yellow onions, finely chopped
1 teaspoon coriander
1 teaspoon curry
1 teaspoon salt
½ teaspoon freshly ground black pepper
2 medium cloves garlic, pressed
1 tablespoon soy sauce

¾ cup shrimp, shelled and deveined
3 eggs

Sauce
4 tablespoons peanut butter
3 tablespoons milk
2 tablespoons soy sauce
½ to 1½ teaspoons Tabasco sauce
1 teaspoon corn syrup

Brown pork and onion in some oil in the wok; cover and continue to fry on very low heat for 10 minutes. Add coriander, curry, salt, black pepper, garlic, and soy sauce. Mix thoroughly. Let fry slowly for another 10 minutes. Add the shrimp and let them get warm.

Meanwhile, beat eggs and stir them into wok. Let simmer for 1 minute and remove from heat. Serve with boiled rice and sauce.

To make sauce, beat peanut butter rapidly with milk and soy sauce. Keep these ingredients cold. Add Tabasco sauce and corn syrup. Makes about 6 servings.

Sub Gum

Chinese Pork

¾ pound pork shoulder
1 (1-pound) can bean sprouts
¼ cup almonds or walnuts, blanched
1 tablespoon soy sauce
2 tablespoons chicken stock or water and bouillon cube

1 level teaspoon sugar
2 tablespoons oil
2 spring onions, thinly sliced
1 pineapple ring, chopped
Salt and pepper

Cut pork into 1/2-inch cubes. Drain bean sprouts, rinse with cold running water, and drain again. Split almonds in half. Mix soy sauce, stock, and sugar together in a small bowl.

Heat oil in wok; add pork and fry, stirring, until browned all over. Stir in almonds and spring onions; fry for 3 to 5 minutes. Drain off any oil. Add remaining ingredients, including bean sprouts; combine thoroughly. Cover pan and cook for 2 minutes. Serve. Makes 4 servings.

Oriental Pork Loin

2 pounds pork loin	½ cup cream
1 red and 1 green pepper	1 small can of vegetable
½ teaspoon curry powder	juice
½ teaspoon paprika powder	Salt
3 tablespoons vegetable oil	Garlic powder
3 tablespoons flour	1 tablespoon mango chutney
1 cup bouillon	2 tablespoons dry white
½ cup milk	wine (if desired)

Cut meat into strips and peppers into small pieces. In the wok, brown curry and paprika in vegetable oil until pungent. Add the flour, bouillon, milk, and cream, stirring constantly.

Add juice, meat, and diced peppers. Simmer for about 5 minutes. Add water, if needed, spices, mango, and wine. Serve with almonds and rice. Makes about 4 servings.

Oriental Pork Stew

1 pound cooked pork, cut into bite-sized pieces	1 teaspoon gingerroot, grated
1 leek or 2 scallions, sliced	½ teaspoon garlic salt
1 small head of cabbage, sliced into ¼-inch slices	1 (8- to 10-ounce) can pineapple slices (4 or 5 slices), cut into pieces
Marinade	Syrup from drained pineapple slices
2 tablespoons vegetable oil	
2 tablespoons soy sauce	

Combine ingredients for marinade in a small bowl. Add pork, cover, and marinate a few hours in refrigerator.

Pour meat and marinade into wok. Add scallions and cabbage. Simmer, covered, for 30 minutes. Serve with boiled rice. Makes 4 servings.

Pork with Peppers and Cashews

1 pound pork, cut into ¾-inch cubes	1 large red (vine-ripened green) pepper, cut into ¾-inch cubes
1 tablespoon soy sauce	1 tablespoon soy sauce
½ teaspoon sugar	1 tablespoon cornstarch in ½ cup cold water or chicken broth
2 tablespoons vegetable oil	
1 small onion, cut into ¾-inch cubes	4 ounces cashews
1 large green pepper, cut into ¾-inch cubes	

Sweet-and-Sour Pork

Combine pork, soy sauce, and sugar and let sit while vegetables are prepared. Heat oil in wok and stir-fry pork mixture for 4 to 5 minutes, until the pork is well done; push aside. Stir-fry onion 1 to 2 minutes, add green peppers, and continue to stir-fry for 2 to 3 minutes. Return pork and add combined soy sauce and cornstarch mixture. Heat and stir gently until sauce is thickened and clear. Add cashews and allow them to heat through. Serve at once with rice. Makes 4 servings.

Sesame Pork with Sweet-and-Sour Vegetables

1 **pound lean pork, cut into ¾-inch pieces**	½ **cup vinegar**
⅓ **cup soy sauce**	½ **cup brown sugar**
⅓ **cup dry sherry**	2 **teaspoons soy sauce**
1 **clove garlic, crushed**	2 **tablespoons cornstarch in ¼ cup water**
	1 **(8-ounce) can water chestnuts, drained and sliced**
Frying Batter	1 **(15¼-ounce) can pineapple chunks, drained**
1 **egg**	
¼ **cup flour**	2 **green peppers, cut into ½-inch cubes**
¼ **cup cornstarch**	2 **cooked carrots, quartered lengthwise and cut into 2-inch lengths**
½ **cup water**	
2 **cups oil for frying**	
	1 **tablespoon toasted sesame seeds**
Sauce	
1 **cup chicken broth**	
½ **cup reserved syrup from pineapple chunks**	

Combine pork, soy sauce, sherry, and garlic. Marinate for 2 hours in refrigerator. Drain. Combine batter ingredients and beat just until smooth. Let stand for 1 hour. Dip pork a few pieces at a time into batter. Drain. Deep-fry in wok at 375°F until pork is done and batter coating is a light, golden brown. Drain on paper towels and keep warm. (If you wish, you may precook the pork.)

Combine broth, reserved pineapple syrup, vinegar, brown sugar, and soy sauce. Heat until sugar dissolves. Add cornstarch mixture and cook until mixture thickens. Add pork, water chestnuts, pineapple, peppers, and carrots. Heat until ingredients are heated through. Serve on chow mein noodles immediately, before crisp batter on the pork softens. Garnish with sesame seeds. Makes 4 servings.

Pork with Oyster Sauce

1 **pound lean pork, cut into 1-inch cubes**	2 **tablespoons oyster sauce**
3 **scallions, cut into ½-inch slices**	1 **tablespoon sherry**
	½ **teaspoon salt**
½ **cup chicken broth**	1 **tablespoon brown sugar**
2 **tablespoons soy sauce**	1 **clove garlic, crushed**
	1 **slice fresh gingerroot**

Combine all ingredients in the wok. Cover and simmer for 15 minutes or until pork is done. Uncover and boil away excess liquid until only 1/2 cup remains. Remove ginger slice. Serve with a stir-fried vegetable and boiled rice. Makes 4 servings.

Chicken with Almonds and Mushrooms

Sub Gum ("Many Costly Things")

2 tablespoons vegetable oil	4 or 5 water chestnuts, sliced
½ pound pork, cut into thin strips	2 cups bean sprouts
2 cloves garlic, crushed	*Sauce*
2 chicken-breast halves, skinned, boned, and cut into thin slices	5 tablespoons soy sauce
	3 tablespoons dry sherry
	2 tablespoons water
½ pound boiled ham, cut into thin slices	1½ tablespoons cornstarch
½ pound shrimp, shelled and deveined	1 teaspoon sugar
	¼ teaspoon pepper
1 small can bamboo shoots, sliced	

Heat oil in wok and stir-fry pork for 6 minutes. Add garlic, chicken, and ham; stir-fry 3 minutes. Add shrimp, bamboo shoots; and water chestnuts. Heat for 3 minutes.

Combine sauce ingredients and add to wok. Heat until sauce is thickened. Add bean sprouts and continue heating 1 to 2 minutes, until they appear wilted. Serve at once. Makes 4 servings.

Spicy Chunking Pork

1 slice gingerroot	6 to 8 Chinese black mushrooms, soaked 30 minutes in water and thinly sliced
2 tablespoons vegetable oil	
1 pound pork, boiled 1 hour and very thinly sliced	
1 (8-ounce) can bamboo shoots, thinly sliced	3 tablespoons dry sherry
	3 tablespoons hoisin sauce
10 to 12 water chestnuts, sliced	1 cup sliced almonds or whole cashews

Brown ginger slice in the hot oil. Remove and discard slice. Add pork and stir-fry 2 minutes. Add bamboo shoots, water chestnuts, and mushrooms; stir-fry 2 minutes. Add sherry and hoisin sauce; stir and heat well. Add nuts. Serve at once with rice. Makes 4 servings.

Pork and Spring Onions

2 tablespoons vegetable oil	1 teaspoon sugar
½ pound pork (butt or shoulder), trimmed and cut into thin strips across the grain	1 teaspoon chili sauce
	8 scallions, cut in quarters lengthwise, then into 4-inch lengths
½ cup chicken broth	
2 tablespoons tomato paste	

Heat oil in wok and stir-fry pork strips 5 to 10 minutes, until crisp and golden. Combine remaining ingredients and add to pork. Simmer for 1 to 2 minutes. Serve at once. Makes 2 servings.

Easy Chicken of the Islands

Sweet-and-Sour Pork

1   pound pork (shoulder or butt) cut into small, bite-sized pieces

Batter
1   large egg
¾   cup water
1   cup all-purpose flour, sifted
½   teaspoon salt
2   cups oil for frying

Vegetables
1   large onion, cut into 8 wedges and separated into layers

1   carrot, sliced diagonally into ⅛-inch slices
2   green peppers, cut into 1-inch squares

Sweet-and-Sour Sauce
2   tablespoons sugar
2   tablespoons soy sauce
2   tablespoons dry sherry
2   tablespoons vinegar
1   tablespoon cornstarch in 2 tablespoons cold water
1   cup cubed canned pineapple, well drained

Prepare batter for pork by combining egg with water. Beat in flour and salt until batter is smooth; allow to stand about 1 hour. (Flour particles will take up some of the water.) Heat oil in wok to 400°F. Dip pork into batter a few pieces at a time and place into the deep fat. Cook for 5 minutes, until cooked through and golden brown. Drain on paper towels, leave uncovered, and keep warm.

Combine onion, carrot slices, and green peppers. Stir-fry in a small amount of oil for 2 to 3 minutes. Combine ingredients for sweet-and-sour sauce and stir until cornstarch is well distributed. Add all at once to the vegetables. Add pineapple chunks and heat until sauce boils and thickens. Pour over pork and serve at once while batter on pork is still crisp. Makes 4 servings.

Twice-Cooked Szechwan Pork

1   pound lean pork
2   tablespoons vegetable oil
1   large green pepper, cut into ¼-inch strips
1   scallion, sliced
1   teaspoon gingerroot, grated
1   clove garlic, grated
1   tablespoon black bean sauce

2   tablespoons water
2   tablespoons hoisin sauce
1   tablespoon dry sherry
¼ to ½ teaspoon chili paste (hot!)
1   teaspoon sugar
½   teaspoon salt

Cover pork with water and simmer, covered, for 1 hour, until done. Cool and slice into 1/4-inch slices. Heat oil in wok and stir-fry green pepper for 1 minute. Add pork and scallion and continue to stir-fry for 1 minute. Combine remaining ingredients and add to pork-and-green pepper mixture. Heat thoroughly and serve at once with boiled or fried rice. Makes 4 servings.

Javanese Chicken Casserole

Poultry

Chicken with Almonds and Mushrooms

2 tablespoons vegetable oil
¼ cup whole blanched almonds
1 green pepper, cut into ½-inch cubes
1 medium onion, cut into ½-inch cubes
¼ pound mushrooms, sliced in "T" shapes
4 chicken-breast halves, skinned, boned, and cut into ½-inch cubes

4 to 5 water chestnuts, sliced
2 teaspoons soy sauce
2 teaspoons dry sherry (or white wine)
½ cup chicken broth or water
1 tablespoon cornstarch in 2 tablespoons cold water

Heat oil in wok and stir-fry almonds until lightly browned. Remove from pan. Stir-fry green pepper and onion 2 to 3 minutes. Push aside. Stir-fry mushrooms 1 to 2 minutes. Push aside. Stir-fry chicken 3 to 4 minutes, until done. Return vegetables to chicken; add water chestnuts.

In a small bowl, combine soy sauce, sherry, chicken broth, and cornstarch mixture. Stir and add to ingredients in wok. Heat until sauce is thickened. Add almonds; serve at once with noodles. Makes 4 servings.

Chicken with Bean Sprouts and Snow Pea Pods

4   chicken-breast halves, skinned, boned, and cut into bite-sized pieces
¼   cup white wine (or dry sherry)
½   teaspoon salt
2   tablespoons vegetable oil
2   cups fresh bean sprouts

1   cup snow pea pods, strings removed
½   teaspoon salt
½   cup chicken broth
1   tablespoon cornstarch in 2 tablespoons water
Sesame seeds, toasted (optional)

Combine chicken, wine, and 1/2 teaspoon salt. Let stand about 20 minutes. Heat oil in wok and stir-fry bean sprouts 1 minute; push aside. Stir-fry pea pods 1 to 2 minutes, until their green color intensifies; push aside. Add chicken and wine mixture and stir-fry 3 to 4 minutes, until chicken is done. Return bean sprouts and pea pods to chicken in wok.

Add combined 1/2 teaspoon salt, chicken broth, and cornstarch mixture. Heat and stir gently until mixture thickens. Serve at once garnished with sesame seeds. Makes 4 servings.

Chicken Bits Oriental

2   tablespoons vegetable oil
2   whole chicken breasts, boned and cubed
¼   cup chicken bouillon
3   tablespoons sherry
1   tablespoon soy sauce
½   teaspoon ginger
½   cup water chestnuts, drained and thinly sliced
¼   cup bamboo shoots, thinly sliced

½   cup pineapple chunks, drained
1   cup frozen peas
3   tablespoons reserved pineapple liquid
2   teaspoons cornstarch
2   tablespoons hoisin sauce
1   tablespoon scallion, minced

Heat vegetable oil in wok. Add chicken cubes and sauté over high heat until evenly browned.

Add chicken bouillon, sherry, soy sauce, ginger, water chestnuts, bamboo shoots, pineapple chunks, and peas. Stir to mix well, then cook over medium heat, stirring constantly, for 2 minutes.

Mix pineapple liquid and cornstarch together well. Add to chicken mixture. Add hoisin sauce, mix well, and cook, stirring constantly, until sauce thickens. Sprinkle with scallions before serving. Makes 3 to 4 servings.

Chicken with Asparagus

2   tablespoons vegetable oil
1   clove garlic
1   pound asparagus, cut
    diagonally into ½-inch
    slices (discard tough,
    white portions)
4   chicken breasts, boned,
    skinned, and cut into ¾-
    inch cubes

1   tablespoon dry sherry
2   tablespoons black bean
    sauce (optional)
1   tablespoon cornstarch in ½
    cup cold chicken broth
1   teaspoon salt

Heat oil in wok and brown garlic to flavor oil. Remove and discard garlic. Stir-fry asparagus 2 to 3 minutes; push aside. Stir-fry chicken 3 to 4 minutes, until done. Return asparagus to wok.

Combine sherry, bean sauce, cornstarch mixture, and salt. Add to chicken and asparagus and heat until sauce thickens. Serve at once with rice or noodles. Makes 4 servings.

Deep-Fried Chicken with Lemon Sauce

4   chicken-breast halves,
    skinned, boned, and cut
    into ½-inch strips

Frying Batter
1   large egg
¾   cup water
1   cup all-purpose flour,
    sifted
2   cups vegetable oil for deep
    frying

Lemon Sauce
1   cup chicken broth
¼   cup dry white wine
1   tablespoon soy sauce
1   tablespoon honey
Grated rind of 1 lemon
3   tablespoons lemon juice
1   tablespoon cornstarch
Lemon slices for garnish

Combine ingredients for frying batter and allow to stand for 1 hour. Dip chicken strips in batter and deep-fry in oil at 400°F a few strips at a time until light golden in color and chicken is done. Use a deep-fat thermometer and control temperature of oil carefully. Remove chicken from oil with a slotted spoon and drain on paper towels.

Combine ingredients for lemon sauce in a small saucepan. Stir constantly and bring to a boil over moderate heat. Simmer 1 to 2 minutes. Arrange chicken in a serving bowl and cover with sauce. Garnish with lemon slices. Serve at once while batter coating is still crisp. Makes 4 servings.

Mandarin Combination

Chicken with Celery and Mushrooms

2 tablespoons vegetable oil	½ cup chicken broth or water
3 to 4 stalks celery, cut into ¼-inch slices	1 tablespoon soy sauce
¼ pound whole small mushrooms	1 tablespoon cornstarch in 2 tablespoons water
1 broiler-fryer chicken, skinned, boned, and cut into ½-inch strips	¼ cup dry sherry

Heat oil in wok and stir-fry celery and mushrooms 2 to 3 minutes; push aside. Stir-fry chicken 3 to 4 minutes or until done. Combine chicken and vegetables. Add broth, soy sauce, cornstarch mixture, and sherry. Heat until sauce boils and is thickened, stirring constantly. Serve at once with rice. Makes 4 servings.

Easy Chicken of the Islands

1   (2- to 3-pound) frying
    chicken, cut into serving
    pieces
½   cup vinegar

½   cup soy sauce
1   clove garlic, finely minced
Dash of freshly ground black
    pepper

Put vinegar, soy sauce, garlic, and pepper in wok. Add chicken; allow this to marinate at least 30 minutes.

After chicken has marinated, heat on top of stove until it comes to a boil. Then cover skillet, lower heat, and allow to simmer about 40 minutes. The liquid will be absorbed into the chicken.

This may be served either hot or cold. Makes 4 to 6 servings.

Javanese Chicken Casserole

2   pounds chicken breasts
1   pound chicken livers
1½ teaspoons flour
Salt and pepper
3   tablespoons margarine or
    butter
1   pound small onions

1   green paprika
½   can bamboo sprouts
3 to 4 slices of canned
    pineapple
1   teaspoon ginger
2   teaspoons brown sugar
2   teaspoons wine vinegar

Cut chicken breasts into even pieces. Do the same with the livers. Coat breast and liver pieces in flour combined with salt and pepper. Brown pieces in a little more than 1/2 of the margarine or butter in a wok. Transfer to a casserole.

Brown onions in rest of the melted fat, allowing the paprika to fry with the onions for a few minutes; then transfer all to the casserole. Whisk the wok with some water and pour into casserole. Add well-drained bamboo sprouts, slices of pineapple, and seasonings. Simmer dish under cover for about 20 minutes.

Meanwhile boil rice to be served with the dish. Beer or red wine is a good beverage with this dish. Makes about 4 servings.

Spicy Chicken and Pineapple

Mandarin Combination

2 tablespoons oil	1½ tablespoons soy sauce
1 medium onion, chopped	¼ pound whole shrimp, cooked
2 cloves garlic, minced	
1 green pepper, cut into ¼ × 1-inch strips	1 cucumber, sliced lengthwise, unpeeled
¼ pound cooked pork or chicken, shredded	2-egg omelet, cut into ½-inch strips
2 cups cold, boiled rice	

Heat oil in wok and add onion, garlic, and green pepper. Stir-fry 1 to 2 minutes. Add cooked meat and stir-fry 1 to 2 minutes. Add rice, soy sauce, and shrimp. Continue to stir-fry until all ingredients are thoroughly heated.

Cut the lengthwise cucumber slices crosswise every 1/4-inch but not all the way through. They will hang together like a comb. Insert them throughout the dish. Garnish with strips of egg omelet. Makes 4 servings.

Chicken with Mushrooms (Moo Goo Gai Pan)

4 chicken-breast halves, boned, skinned, and cut into ½-inch cubes	¼ pound mushrooms, sliced into "T" shapes
	6 water chestnuts, sliced
¼ cup dry white wine	½ cup chicken broth
½ teaspoon salt	1 tablespoon cornstarch in 2 tablespoons cold water
2 scallions, cut into ½-inch slices	
½ cup celery, cut into ½-inch cubes	½ teaspoon salt
	Whole, blanched almonds (optional)
1 tablespoon vegetable oil	
12 snow pea pods, strings removed	

Combine chicken with wine and 1/2 teaspoon salt; set aside. Stir-fry scallions and celery in oil for 1 minute; push aside. Stir-fry snow pea pods 2 minutes; push aside. Stir-fry mushrooms and water chestnuts 1 to 2 minutes; push aside. Add chicken and wine and stir-fry 2 to 3 minutes, until chicken is done. Combine chicken and vegetables in wok.

Stir the broth, cornstarch mixture, and another 1/2 teaspoon salt together. Add slowly to the chicken and vegetables in the wok and heat until thickened and clear. Serve over rice and sprinkle with almonds, if desired. Makes 4 servings.

Sweet-and-Sour Chicken with Cucumbers and Cantaloupe

Chicken with Hoisin Sauce

4	chicken-breast halves, boned, skinned, and cut into ¾-inch cubes	1	tablespoon vegetable oil
1	tablespoon cornstarch	½	pound mushrooms, cut into ½-inch cubes
1	tablespoon dry sherry	2½	tablespoons hoisin sauce
1	tablespoon soy sauce	¼	cup cashews
1	green pepper, cut into ½-inch squares		

Sprinkle cubed chicken with cornstarch, dry sherry, and soy sauce. Toss to coat well and set aside. Stir-fry green pepper in oil for 1 minute; push aside. Add mushrooms. Stir-fry for 1 to 2 minutes; push aside. Stir-fry chicken 2 to 3 minutes, until done. Add hoisin sauce and cashews. Reheat, and stir briefly. Serve at once. Makes 4 servings.

Oriental Chicken with Chinese Mushrooms

2 tablespoons soy sauce
1 tablespoon cornstarch
1 whole broiler-fryer chicken, boned, skinned, and cut into bite-sized pieces
1 clove garlic, halved lengthwise
2 slices gingerroot, 1/8 inch thick
2 tablespoons vegetable oil
1/2 pound fresh mushrooms, quartered through the stem and cap
4 or 5 dried black Chinese mushrooms, soaked 30 minutes in warm water, drained, and diced

2 tablespoons black bean sauce or hoisin sauce

Oriental Vegetables
1 tablespoon oil
1/4 cup blanched almonds, slivered
2 green peppers, sliced into 1/4-inch strips (if possible, substitute a yellow pepper for 1 green pepper)
2 scallions, shredded in 2-inch lengths
1 (8-ounce) can bamboo shoots, sliced
Salt

Combine soy sauce and cornstarch in small bowl. Add chicken and marinate 1/2 hour. Brown garlic and ginger slices in oil. Remove and discard garlic and ginger. Stir-fry fresh and black mushrooms 1 to 2 minutes; push aside. Stir-fry chicken 3 to 4 minutes, until done. Add black bean sauce. Stir mushrooms and chicken together and heat through.

Make Oriental vegetables: Heat oil in wok. Stir-fry almonds 1 to 2 minutes, until brown; remove from pan. Stir-fry green peppers, scallions, and bamboo shoots one at a time for 1 to 2 minutes each. Add salt to taste. Add almonds to the vegetables and serve at once. Serve chicken over the vegetables. Makes 4 servings.

Shredded Chicken with Almonds

2 tablespoons vegetable oil
1/4 cup whole, blanched almonds
1 medium onion, chopped
1 teaspoon gingerroot, grated

4 chicken-breast halves, skinned, boned, and sliced into 1/2-inch strips
2 tablespoons soy sauce
1 tablespoon dry sherry
1 teaspoon sugar

Heat oil in wok and stir-fry almonds 1 to 2 minutes, until golden. Remove from pan. Stir-fry onion and ginger 2 to 3 minutes. Add chicken and continue to stir-fry 3 to 4 minutes, until done. Return almonds to pan. Combine soy sauce, sherry, and sugar. Pour over chicken mixture. Heat and serve at once. Makes 4 servings.

Chicken Livers with Eggs and Noodles

Kang Pao Chicken

4   **chicken-breast halves, skinned, boned, and cubed into ¾-inch cubes**
1   **egg white**
1   **tablespoon cornstarch**
2   **tablespoons vegetable oil**
1   **cup unsalted peanuts or cashews**
2   **scallions, sliced**

2   **tablespoons dry sherry**
2   **tablespoons hoisin sauce**
4   **tablespoons black bean sauce**
¼ to ½ **teaspoon chili paste (very hot!)**
1   **tablespoon vinegar**
1   **teaspoon sugar**

Combine cubed chicken with egg white and cornstarch. Refrigerate for 1/2 hour. Heat oil in wok and stir-fry chicken 3 to 4 minutes, until done. Add nuts, scallions, and remaining ingredients. Heat thoroughly and serve at once with rice. Makes 4 servings.

Pineapple Chicken with Sweet-and-Sour Sauce

2   tablespoons vegetable oil
1   green pepper, cut into ¼-inch strips
1   broiler-fryer chicken, skinned, boned, and cut into ½-inch cubes
1   (8-ounce) can pineapple rings, drained and cut into bite-sized pieces

¼   cup dry sherry or white wine
1   tablespoon vinegar
1   tablespoon cornstarch in 2 tablespoons cold water
2   tablespoons orange marmalade
1   tablespoon soy sauce
1   teaspoon gingerroot, grated

Sauce
½   cup chicken broth
¼   cup reserved syrup from canned pineapple

Heat oil in wok and stir-fry green pepper 1 to 2 minutes; push aside. Stir-fry chicken 3 to 4 minutes, until done. Return green peppers to chicken; add pineapple.

Combine sauce ingredients and add to wok. Heat and stir until sauce is thickened and clear. Serve immediately with rice. Makes 4 servings.

Chicken and Shrimp with Vegetables

2   chicken-breast halves, skinned, boned, and cut into ¼-inch strips
1   tablespoon dry sherry
2   tablespoons soy sauce
2   tablespoons oil
2   cups mixed vegetables (green beans, sliced mushrooms, strips of green pepper, shredded carrots, etc.)
½   cup chicken broth
1   tablespoon cornstarch in 2 tablespoons cold water

½   pound cooked whole shrimp
8   ounces thin spaghetti noodles, cooked according to package directions and tossed with 1 tablespoon soy sauce
1   egg, beaten and cooked in a small skillet over moderate heat as an omelet

Marinate chicken in sherry and soy sauce for about 20 minutes. Heat oil in wok and stir-fry vegetables for 2 to 3 minutes; push aside. Add chicken and stir-fry for 3 to 4 minutes, until done. Return vegetables to chicken in wok. Add broth, cornstarch mixture, and cooked shrimp. Heat until sauce boils and shrimp are heated through.

Serve over spaghetti noodles and garnish with the 1-egg omelet, cut into 1/4 inch strips. Makes 4 servings.

Chicken Livers with Peanuts

Spicy Chicken and Pineapple

1 (3-pound) chicken	3 tablespoons oil
¾ level teaspoon chili powder	1 (12-ounce) can pineapple pieces, drained
1 level teaspoon salt	2 level teaspoons lemon rind, grated
3 cloves garlic, crushed	2 tablespoons lemon juice
10 spring onions, thinly sliced	1 cup coconut milk (see below)
2 level teaspoons tomato puree	2 teaspoons soy sauce

Cut chicken meat from bone and chop into 1-inch pieces. In a large bowl, mix chili powder, salt, garlic, spring onions (reserve a few slices for garnish), and tomato puree together. Add chicken pieces, mix well; and leave for at least 1 hour.

Heat oil in wok and fry chicken and pineapple until chicken is lightly browned. Add lemon rind and juice, coconut milk, and soy sauce. Cover and simmer very gently for 30 minutes or until chicken is tender. Serve immediately, garnished with the few reserved spring onion slices and accompanied by freshly cooked rice and hot spicy chutney.

To make coconut milk: Place 1 can (6 to 8 ounces) desiccated coconut in a saucepan with 2 cups water. Bring to a boil, then cover pan and remove it from heat. When lukewarm, strain milk through several thicknesses of cheesecloth. Makes 4 to 6 servings.

Stewed Chicken with Pork

1 clove garlic	4 tablespoons soy sauce
1 small slice of fresh gingerroot	3 teaspoons sugar
8 ounces pork, cut into 1-inch cubes	3 tablespoons dry sherry
	Water—barely enough to cover ingredients
8 ounces chicken, cut into 1-inch cubes	1 tablespoon cornstarch in 2 tablespoons cold water (optional)
2 tablespoons cooking oil	

Brown garlic, ginger, pork, and chicken in 2 tablespoons of cooking oil over medium-high heat. Add soy sauce, sugar, sherry, and sufficient water to cover meat.

Cover and simmer over low heat for about an hour or until meat is tender. Remove ginger and garlic clove. Serve meat hot with the sauce. If you wish, sauce may be thickened by adding 1 tablespoon of cornstarch in 2 tablespoons of cold water to the sauce. Heat until sauce thickens and is clear. Makes 3 to 4 servings.

Soy Sauce Chicken

1 (4½- to 5-pound) roasting chicken	1 whole star anise, or 8 sections star anise
2 cups cold water	¼ cup rock candy in small pieces, or 2 tablespoons granulated sugar
2 cups soy sauce	
¼ cup Chinese rice wine, or pale dry sherry	1 teaspoon sesame seed oil
5 slices peeled, fresh gingerroot, about 1 inch in diameter and ⅛ inch thick	

Wash chicken and dry with paper towels. In a wok large enough to hold chicken snugly, bring water, soy sauce, wine, ginger, and star anise to a boil, then add the chicken. The liquid should reach halfway up the chicken. Bring to boil, reduce heat to moderate, and cook covered for 20 minutes. Turn chicken over. Stir rock candy or sugar into sauce and baste chicken thoroughly. Simmer 20 minutes longer, basting frequently. Turn off heat, cover wok, and let chicken cook for 2 to 3 hours.

Transfer chicken to chopping board and brush it with sesame seed oil. Remove wings and legs and split chicken in half lengthwise by cutting through its breastbone and backbone. Lay halves skin-side-up on the board and chop them crosswise, bones and all, into 1 × 3-inch pieces, reconstructing the pieces in approximately their original shape in the center of a platter as you proceed. Chop wings and legs similarly and place them around breasts. Moisten chicken with 1/4 cup of the sauce in which it cooked and serve at room temperature. Makes 4 to 6 servings.

Chicken with Walnuts

4 chicken-breast halves, skinned, boned, and cut into ¾-inch cubes	1 clove garlic, grated
3 tablespoons soy sauce	½ cup chicken broth or water
1 teaspoon sugar	1 tablespoon cornstarch in 2 tablespoons cold water
2 tablespoons vegetable oil	
1 cup English walnuts	1 (8-ounce) can bamboo shoots, drained and sliced
1 teaspoon gingerroot, grated	

Marinate chicken in soy sauce and sugar in a small bowl for 20 minutes. Heat oil in wok and stir-fry walnuts 2 minutes. Remove from pan. Add chicken, ginger, garlic, and marinade to wok and stir-fry 3 to 4 minutes, until chicken is done. Combine broth and cornstarch mixture. Add to chicken along with bamboo shoots. Heat and stir gently until sauce is thickened and bamboo shoots are hot. Add walnuts and serve at once with rice. Makes 4 servings.

Sweet-and-Sour Chicken with Cucumbers and Cantaloupe

4   chicken-breast halves,
     skinned, boned, and cut
     into bite-sized cubes
1½   tablespoons soy sauce
1   tablespoon dry sherry
1   tablespoon cornstarch
2   tablespoons vegetable oil
1   cucumber, cut into bite-
     sized cubes after the skin
     has been scored
     lengthwise with the tines
     of a fork (seeds may be
     removed)
¼ to ½ cantaloupe, seeded,
     rind removed, and cut into
     bite-sized pieces

1   sweet red pepper (if
     available), cubed
2   ounces blanched, whole
     almonds

Sauce
3   tablespoons brown sugar
3   tablespoons vinegar
½   cup pineapple juice
1   teaspoon soy sauce
1   tablespoon cornstarch in 2
     tablespoons cold water

Marinate chicken cubes in combined soy sauce, dry sherry, and corn-starch while remaining ingredients are being prepared. Heat oil in wok and stir-fry chicken mixture for 3 to 4 minutes. Add cucumber, cantaloupe, and red pepper (if used).

Combine ingredients for sweet-and-sour sauce and add these to wok. Stir gently and heat until sauce boils and cucumber and melon are heated through. Serve at once garnished with almonds. Makes 4 servings.

Chicken Livers with Eggs and Noodles

4   eggs
¼   teaspoon salt
1   tablespoon vegetable oil
½   pound mushrooms, sliced
     in "T" shapes
2   scallions, sliced
1   pound chicken livers,
     cubed

2   tablespoons dry sherry
5   tablespoons soy sauce
½   pound thin spaghetti
     noodles
2   tablespoons parsley,
     chopped

Combine eggs and salt; pour into an oiled skillet. Cook without stirring over moderate heat until eggs are set. Cut into 1/2-inch cubes.

Heat oil in wok. Stir-fry mushrooms and scallions 1 to 2 minutes; push aside. Stir-fry chicken livers 1 to 2 minutes. Add dry sherry and 4 table-spoons soy sauce. Combine liver and vegetables; heat through. Add cubed eggs.

Steamed Sea Bass

Prepare spaghetti according to package directions; drain well and gently combine with 1 tablespoon soy sauce. Serve on a platter with the liver mixture. Garnish with chopped parsley. Makes 4 servings.

Fish Tempura

Chicken Livers with Peanuts

2 tablespoons oil	½ teaspoon gingerroot, finely chopped
1 can bamboo shoots, drained and sliced	½ level teaspoon salt
¼ cup peanuts	1 level tablespoon brown sugar
½ pound chicken livers	½ cup chicken stock or water and chicken stock cube
2 spring onions, finely chopped	1 level tablespoon cornstarch
2 tablespoons soy sauce	
1 clove garlic, crushed	

Heat the oil in a wok and fry the bamboo shoots and peanuts, stirring frequently for about 5 minutes. Remove and drain on absorbent kitchen paper. Add the chicken livers to the pan and fry gently until golden brown all over. Remove from the wok and drain.

Place the spring onions, soy sauce, garlic, ginger, salt, sugar and stock in the wok. Blend the cornstarch with a little liquid in a small bowl and stir it into the wok. Bring to a boil, stirring, and simmer for 2 to 3 minutes. Return the livers to the pan and reheat. Serve in a heated dish, sprinkled with the peanuts and bamboo shoots. Makes 4 servings.

Seafood

Deep-Fried Fish with Sweet-and-Sour Sauce

1½ to 2 pounds fish fillets
Salt

Batter for Frying
1½ cups biscuit mix
1 cup water
2 eggs
¾ teaspoon salt
2 cups oil for frying

Sauce
1 cup water
½ cup cider vinegar
6 tablespoons catsup
2 cups brown sugar
2 teaspoons soy sauce
2 tablespoons cornstarch
1 tablespoon sesame seeds, toasted in the oven on a baking sheet until light brown

Cut fish into 1-inch cubes or 1/2-inch strips. Salt lightly. Combine ingredients for the batter and stir until smooth and free of lumps. Dip fish pieces into batter and deep-fry at 375°F until golden brown, turning once. Drain on paper towels and keep warm, uncovered.

Combine ingredients for the sauce in a small saucepan. Stir constantly over moderate heat until mixture thickens. Pour over fish. Sprinkle with sesame seeds. Serve at once while batter coating is still crisp. Makes 4 to 6 servings.

Steamed Fish with Scallions and Ginger

2 tablespoons vinegar	1 teaspoon salt
2 cups water	1 teaspoon fresh gingerroot, grated
2 teaspoons whole pickling spices	3 tablespoons scallions, minced
1 to 1½ pounds fish fillets (flounder, perch, etc.)	

Combine vinegar, water, and pickling spices in wok. Place fish on a metal rack 1 to 2 inches above the vinegar and water, so the water will not boil up onto the fish but steam can circulate freely around it. Combine salt, ginger, and scallions and spread evenly over surface of the fillets.

Place lid on wok and steam for 10 to 20 minutes, or just until fish will separate into flakes with a fork. Serve immediately. (The vinegar and spices in the cooking water eliminate the characteristic odor in the kitchen of cooked fish.) Makes 4 servings.

Lobster Cantonese

2 tablespoons vegetable oil	1 cup chicken broth or water
2 tablespoons black beans, rinsed and mashed	1 teaspoon soy sauce
2 cloves garlic, grated	½ teaspoon sugar
1 teaspoon gingerroot, grated	1 tablespoon cornstarch in 2 tablespoons cold water
2 to 3 ounces pork, minced or ground	Salt and pepper
1½ to 2 pounds live lobster, cleaned and chopped into 1-inch pieces or 1 pound lobster tails, split lengthwise	1 egg, beaten
	1 scallion, sliced

Heat oil in wok and brown black beans, garlic, and ginger briefly. Add pork and stir-fry for 1 minute. Add lobster and stir-fry for 1 minute. Add broth, soy sauce, sugar, and cornstarch mixture. Cover and heat for 5 minutes.

Remove from heat, season with salt and pepper, and slowly pour in the egg while stirring with a fork. This sauce should not be so hot as to completely coagulate the egg and turn it white. The egg should give the sauce a yellowish color. Serve at once with rice. Garnish with scallion slices. Makes 4 servings.

Steamed Fish with Black Bean Sauce

2 tablespoons black bean sauce	1 teaspoon vegetable oil (for non-oily fish)
1 clove garlic, grated	2 cups water
1 teaspoon fresh gingerroot, grated	1 to 1½ pounds fish fillets (flounder, trout, etc.)
½ teaspoon sugar	1 scallion, sliced

Combine bean sauce, garlic, ginger, sugar, and oil. Place 2 cups water in wok and arrange fish on a rack 1 to 2 inches above water, so the water will not boil up onto the fish but steam can circulate freely around it. Spread bean sauce mixture evenly over surface of the fillets. Sprinkle with scallion slices.

Cover wok and steam until fish separates into flakes with a fork. Serve immediately. (Rack may be covered with a layer of cheesecloth before fish are placed on it. This will prevent fish from adhering to the rack.) Makes 4 servings.

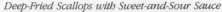

Deep-Fried Scallops with Sweet-and-Sour Sauce

Steamed Sea Bass

2 **sea bass, about 1½ pounds each, cleaned but with heads and tails left on**	1 **scallion, including the green top, cut into 2-inch lengths**
1 **teaspoon salt**	1 **tablespoon vegetable oil**
4 **mushrooms, chopped**	½ **teaspoon sugar**
1 **tablespoon soy sauce**	2 **whole shrimp**
1 **tablespoon dry sherry**	
1 **tablespoon fresh gingerroot, peeled and finely shredded**	

Wash bass with cold water and dry with paper towels. With a sharp knife, make diagonal cuts 1/4 inch deep at 1/2-inch intervals on both sides of each fish. Sprinkle fish, inside and out, with salt.

Lay fish on a heatproof platter 1/2 inch smaller in diameter than the bamboo steamer. Pour chopped mushrooms and seasonings over fish, and arrange pieces of ginger and scallion on top.

Pour enough boiling water into lower part of wok so that it comes within an inch of the bamboo steamer. Bring water to a rolling boil and place platter of fish into steamer with shrimp arranged as shown in the picture. Steam fish for about 15 minutes, or until they are firm to the touch. Serve at once in their own steaming platter. Makes 4 servings.

Fish Tempura

2 **pounds fresh fish fillets**	2 **cups ice water**
Salt to taste	**Oil**
Lemon juice	**Soy sauce**

Basic Tempura Batter	*Chili-Horseradish Sauce*
2 **cups all-purpose flour, sifted**	1 **cup mayonnaise**
3 **egg yolks**	⅓ **cup chili sauce**
	3 **tablespoons horseradish**

Cut fish fillets into bite-sized pieces and drain well on paper towels. Prepare other ingredients. Season fish with salt and squeeze desired amount of lemon juice over fish.

Make up tempura batter. Sift flour 3 times. Combine yolks and water in a large bowl over ice and beat with a whisk until well blended. Gradually add flour, stirring and turning the mixture with a spoon. Don't overmix. Keep batter over ice while frying. Makes approximately 4-1/2 cups; use 1/2 the batter for this recipe.

Place all fish in the batter. When ready to fry, remove fish from batter with a fork and drain slightly. Heat oil in a wok to between 350 and 375°F.

Fry fish, a few pieces at a time, for about 5 minutes, turning to brown evenly. Remove fish from oil with a slotted spoon and drain well on paper towels. Keep fish warm until all is cooked. Serve dipped into soy sauce or with chili-horseradish sauce. Makes 4 servings.

To make chili-horseradish sauce, combine all ingredients in small bowl and mix thoroughly. Chill well before serving. Makes approximately 1-1/2 cups.

Shrimp with Bean Sprouts

1 green pepper (or a red, ripe one), cut into ¼-inch strips	2 teaspoons soy sauce Salt
1 cup bean sprouts	*Crispy Fried Noodles*
1 teaspoon gingerroot, grated	12 ounces fine egg noodles
2 tablespoons vegetable oil	2 cups vegetable oil for frying
6 ounces cooked shrimp	
1 tablespoon dry sherry	

Combine green pepper, bean sprouts, and ginger. Heat oil; stir-fry vegetables about 2 minutes. Push aside. Add shrimp; stir-fry until heated. Combine shrimp and vegetables; add sherry and soy sauce. Salt to taste. Serve hot with crispy fried noodles.

To make noodles, cook them in boiling, salted water according to package directions. Drain; rinse thoroughly in cold water. Dry on paper towels. Fry handfuls of noodles in oil at 375°F, turning frequently, about 5 minutes. Drain on paper towels. Makes 4 servings.

Butterfly Shrimp

1½ pounds large shrimp, cleaned and deveined, with tails left on	½ teaspoon salt
	¾ cup milk
¾ cup flour	1 egg, beaten
1 teaspoon baking powder	Fat for frying

Cut almost through shrimp lengthwise; spread out to form the butterfly.

Mix flour, baking powder, and salt with milk and beaten egg. Stir until very smooth. Heat fat in wok. Dip each shrimp in batter; put into hot fat. Fry until golden brown, about 7 minutes. Drain cooked shrimp on paper towels. Makes 4 to 6 servings.

Deep-Fried Scallops with Sweet-and-Sour Sauce

1 pound scallops (cubed fish fillets may be substituted)	Reserved pineapple syrup and water to make 1 cup
	1 tablespoon cornstarch in 2 tablespoons cold water
Batter	
1 cup all-purpose flour, sifted	2 tablespoons vinegar
¾ cup water	¼ cup brown sugar
1 large egg	1 teaspoon soy sauce
½ teaspoon salt	1 small onion, sliced
2 cups oil for frying	Few strips each of carrots and green pepper
Sweet-and-Sour Sauce	2 cups hot boiled rice
4 pineapple rings, cut into small pieces	

Combine batter ingredients and beat just until smooth. Allow to stand for 1 hour. Dip scallops a few at a time into batter and deep-fry in oil at 375°F just until golden brown and done, about 3 to 4 minutes. Drain on paper towels.

Combine sauce ingredients in a saucepan. Stir constantly while bringing to a boil. Heat until thickened and the carrot and pepper strips are heated through.

Place scallops on a bed of boiled rice and cover with sauce. Serve at once while scallop batter coating is still crisp. Makes 4 servings.

Shrimp in Garlic Sauce

2 tablespoons vegetable oil	1 cup peas, fresh or frozen defrosted
1 small onion, chopped	
1 teaspoon gingerroot, grated	1 pound cooked shrimp
4 cloves garlic, sliced	½ cup chicken broth or water
5 or 6 Chinese dried black mushrooms, soaked 30 minutes in warm water and sliced	2 teaspoons soy sauce
	1 teaspoon salt
	1 tablespoon cornstarch in 2 tablespoons water

Heat oil in wok and stir-fry onion, ginger, and garlic for 1 to 2 minutes. Add mushrooms and peas and stir-fry 1 to 3 minutes. Add shrimp and continue to stir-fry 1 to 2 minutes.

Combine broth, soy sauce, salt, and cornstarch mixture. Add to wok and heat until sauce boils and has thickened. Serve immediately with boiled rice. Makes 4 servings.

Shrimp in Garlic Sauce

Shrimp with Lobster Sauce

2	to 3 ounces minced pork	1	cup chicken broth or water
2	tablespoons vegetable oil	1	teaspoon soy sauce
1	pound cooked shrimp, cut into bite-sized pieces	1	teaspoon salt
		1	teaspoon sugar
1	teaspoon gingerroot, grated	2	tablespoons dry sherry
3	cloves garlic, grated	1	tablespoon cornstarch in 2 tablespoons cold water
1	tablespoon black beans (dow sei), washed and mashed	1	egg, beaten
		Scallion slices, leaves only	

Stir-fry pork in vegetable oil until well done. Add shrimp, ginger, garlic, and beans; stir-fry briefly. Combine broth, soy sauce, salt, sugar, sherry, and cornstarch mixture. Stir and add to wok. Heat until thickened. Remove from heat and pour egg in slowly, while stirring with a fork.

Serve on rice and garnish with green scallion slices. The sauce must not be hot enough to coagulate the egg as it is stirred in with a fork. The purpose of the egg is to color the sauce and thicken it slightly. Makes 4 servings.

Oriental Shrimp

1 teaspoon curry Paprika powder	2 pounds shrimp, shelled and deveined
4 tablespoons margarine or butter	6 tablespoons tomato puree
2 red and 2 green paprikas	½ cup water
2 yellow onions or 2 pieces of leek	½ cup dry white wine
	½ cup heavy cream
2 clove garlics or garlic powder	Salt
	2 cups fresh mushrooms

In a wok, fry curry and paprika powder in margarine or butter; add paprika strips, onions, garlic, and shrimp to soften. Add tomato puree, water, wine, and cream and let simmer for a few minutes.

Cook until shrimp are heated through; taste and correct seasoning. Stir in mushrooms and finish cooking. Makes about 4 servings.

Shrimp with Cauliflower and Chicken

1 tablespoon vegetable oil	*Sauce*
1½ cups cauliflower, cut into florets and parboiled (cover with boiling water and let stand 5 minutes)	¾ cup chicken broth
	1 tablespoon soy sauce
	2 tablespoons chili sauce
½ cup peas, fresh, or frozen and defrosted	1 tablespoon cornstarch in 2 tablespoons cold water
½ pound cooked chicken, cubed	2 tablespoons dry white wine
1 pound whole shrimp, cooked	
2 scallions, cut lengthwise into thin strips	

Heat oil in wok; stir-fry cauliflower florets 2 minutes. Remove and reserve. Stir-fry peas 2 minutes; reserve with cauliflower. Add chicken, shrimp, and scallions to wok. Stir-fry 2 to 3 minutes, until heated. Return vegetables to pan.

Combine sauce ingredients; add to pan. Heat until sauce boils and thickens. Serve with rice. Makes 4 servings.

Oriental Shrimp

Shrimp Tempura

1	**pound fresh large shrimp**
8	**ounces bamboo shoots**
4	**peppers, green, red, and yellow**
4	**small onions**
2	**sugared or candied ginger**

Tempura Batter

2	**ounces rice flour**
6	**ounces flour**
1	**cup water**
4	**jiggers rice wine or sherry**
8	**egg whites**

4	**cups oil for frying**

Rinse shrimp. Drain bamboo shoots; cut into 1/2-inch pieces. Cut peppers into 1/2-inch strips. Cut onions into thick slices; separate into rings. Slice sugared ginger. Arrange these ingredients in separate small bowls.

To prepare batter, place both kinds of flour in a bowl. In a separate bowl, combine water, rice wine or sherry, and egg whites until well blended. Gradually stir into flour to form loose batter.

Heat oil in wok. Each person places shrimp or piece of vegetable on a fondue fork, dips it in batter, and deep-fries it in hot oil. Makes 4 servings.

EQUIVALENT MEASURES

dash = 2 or 3 drops
pinch = amount that can be held between ends of thumb & forefinger
1 tablespoon = 3 teaspoons
¼ cup = 4 tablespoons
⅓ cup = 5 tablespoons + 1 teaspoon
½ cup = 8 tablespoons
1 cup = 16 tablespoons
1 pint = 2 cups
1 quart = 4 cups
1 gallon = 4 quarts
1 peck = 8 quarts
1 bushel = 4 pecks
1 pound = 16 ounces

KITCHEN METRIC

measurements you will encounter most often in recipes are: centimeter (cm), milliliter (ml), gram (g), kilogram (kg)

cup equivalents (volume):

¼ cup = 60 ml
⅓ cup = 85 ml
½ cup = 125 ml
⅔ cup = 170 ml
¾ cup = 180 ml
1 cup = 250 ml
1¼ cups = 310 ml
1½ cups = 375 ml
2 cups = 500 ml
3 cups = 750 ml
5 cups = 1250 ml

spoonful equivalents (volume):

⅛ teaspoon = .5 ml
¼ teaspoon = 1.5 ml
½ teaspoon = 3 ml
¾ teaspoon = 4 ml
1 teaspoon = 5 ml
1 tablespoon = 15 ml
2 tablespoons = 30 ml
3 tablespoons = 45 ml

pan sizes (linear & volume):

1 inch = 2.5 cm
8-inch square = 20-cm square
9×13×1½-inch = 20×33×4-cm
10×6×2-inch = 25×15×5-cm
13×9×2-inch = 33×23×5-cm
7½×12×1½-inch = 18×30×4-cm
(above are baking dishes, pans)
9×5×3-inch = 23×13×8-cm
(loaf pan)
10-inch = 25 cm 12-inch = 30-cm
(skillets)
1-quart = 1-liter 2-quart = 2-liter
(baking dishes, by volume)
5- to 6-cup = 1.5-liter
(ring mold)

weight (meat amounts; can & package sizes):

1 ounce = 28 g
½ pound = 225 g
¾ pound = 340 g
1 pound = 450 g
1½ pounds = 675 g
2 pounds = 900 g
3 pounds = 1.4 kg (in recipes, amounts of meat above 2 pounds will generally be stated in kilograms)
10 ounces = 280 g (most frozen vegetables)
10½ ounces = 294 g (most condensed soups)
15 ounces = 425 g (common can size)
16 ounces = 450 g (common can size)
1 pound, 24 ounces = 850 g (can size)

OVEN TEMPERATURES

275°F = 135°C
300°F = 149°C
325°F = 165°C
350°F = 175°C
375°F = 190°C
400°F = 205°C
425°F = 218°C
450°F = 230°C
500°F = 260°C

Note that Celsius temperatures are sometimes rounded off to the nearest reading ending in 0 or 5; the Celsius thermometer is the same as Centigrade, a term no longer used.

Index

Recipe photograph page number in italic.